THE GREAT BRITISH TRAIN ROBBERY, 1963

THE GREAT BRITISH TRAIN ROBBERY, 1963

MOMENTS OF HISTORY

Series editor: Tim Coates

London and New York

Applications for reproduction should be made in writing to Tim Coates, c/o Littlehampton Book Services, Durrington, West Sussex BN13 3RB, UK or c/o Midpoint Trade Books, 27 West 20th Street, Suite 1102, New York, NY 10011, USA.

ISBN 1 84381 022 0
Material held at The National Archives (Public Record Office) under document references HO 242/4 and HO 242/5 reproduced with permission from the Keeper of Public Records.
© Crown copyright
This selection and this edition © Tim Coates.

A CIP catalogue record for this book is available from the British Library.

Editor: Frances Maher
Photographs: Cecilia Weston-Baker
Maps/diagrams: Duncan Stewart
Cover design: David Carroll and Sarah Theodosiou
Design: Sarah Theodosiou
Manufactured in Singapore by Imago
Series Editor: Tim Coates

Cover photograph © Hulton-Deutsch Collection/CORBIS: Ronald Biggs under arrest, October 6, 1963
Inside front cover © Bettmann/CORBIS: Police investigating the hijacked travelling post office, August 8, 1963
Inside back cover © Stuart Westmorland/CORBIS: Statue of Justice

About the series

Moments of History are historic official papers which have not previously been available in a popular form. They have been chosen for the quality of their story-telling and are illustrated with contemporary photographs and drawings. Some subjects are familiar, but others are less well known. Each is a moment in history. A complete list of this and the associate series *uncovered editions* is to be found at the back of this book. Further details are available on www.timcoatesbooks.com.

About the series editor, Tim Coates

Tim Coates studied at University College, Oxford and at the University of Stirling. After working in the theatre for a number of years, he took up bookselling and became managing director, firstly of Sherratt and Hughes bookshops, and then of Waterstone's. He is known for his support for foreign literature, particularly from the Czech Republic, and specializes in the republishing of interesting archives. The idea for *uncovered editions* came while searching through the bookshelves of his late father-in-law, Air Commodore Patrick Cave OBE. Tim Coates is married to Bridget Cave, has two sons and lives in London. He is the author of *The Lady in the Case: The Romances of Patsy Cornwallis West* (published by Bloomsbury in 2003).

Tim Coates welcomes views and ideas on the *Moments of History* and *uncovered editions* series.
He can be e-mailed at timcoatesbooks@yahoo.com.

The publishers would like to thank the photographers and organizations for their kind permission to reproduce the photographs in this book.

Every effort has been made to trace the holders of any copyright material included in this book. However, if there are any omissions we will be happy to rectify them in future editions.

Copyright in illustrations is as follows:

CORBIS, London:
Bettmann – pp. x, 33, 47, 50, 66, 71, 89, 155, 163, 171, 174 (bottom right and left)
Jason Hawkes – p. 11
John Heseltine – p. 146
Hulton-Deutsch Collection – pp. ix, xiv, 2, 43, 63, 77, 121, 124, 131, 137
Arthur W.V. Mace, Milepost 92½ – p. iv
O.S. Nock, Milepost 92½ – p. 22

Hulton | Archive, London – pp. 15, 27, 30, 39, 81, 84, 94, 100, 109, 117, 168, 174 (top right and left)

Rex Features, London:
Chris Bott – p. 172

We are grateful to the Museum of the Bank of England for supplying the images of the banknotes on p. xii.

Police officers on patrol in Aylesbury, Buckinghamshire, c.1955

In the early hours of 8th August 1963, a gang of at least 15 men stopped and attacked the Glasgow to London mail train near Leighton Buzzard in Buckinghamshire. They made off with 120 mailbags containing almost £2.6 million, a huge amount of money in those days. It was the biggest robbery of all time.

The text that follows is an extract from the report (which has been edited to secure anonymity) of Her Majesty's Inspector of Constabulary, submitted to the Home Office in 1964, just over a year after the robbery had taken place. At the time of writing the investigation was not complete: much of the stolen money had not been recovered and at least three criminals were still at large.

A brief postscript covers the later arrest and sentencing of Ronald 'Buster' Edwards, Bruce Reynolds and James White – and the re-arrest of Ronnie Biggs in 2001, 36 years after his escape from prison.

The travelling post office in Cheddington station after the robbery

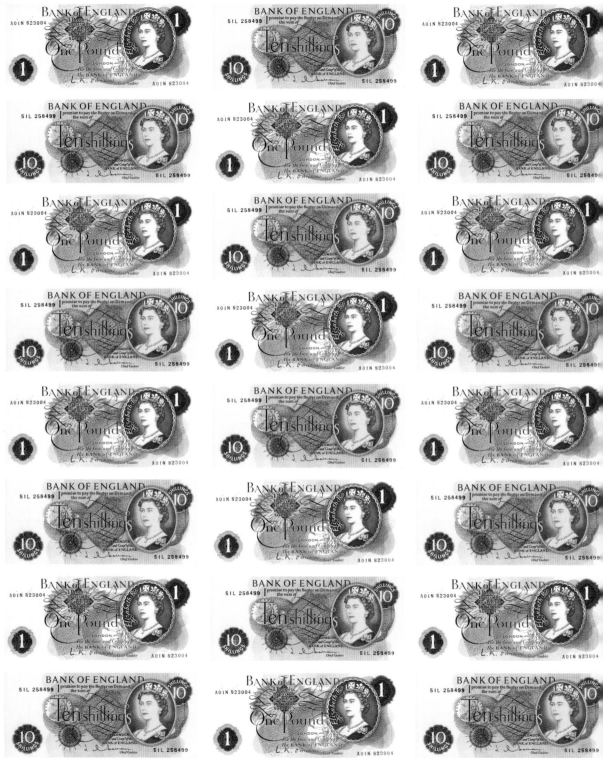

CONTENTS

£1 and 10/- notes current in 1963. The Series C notes were the first to
feature a portrait of the reigning monarch.

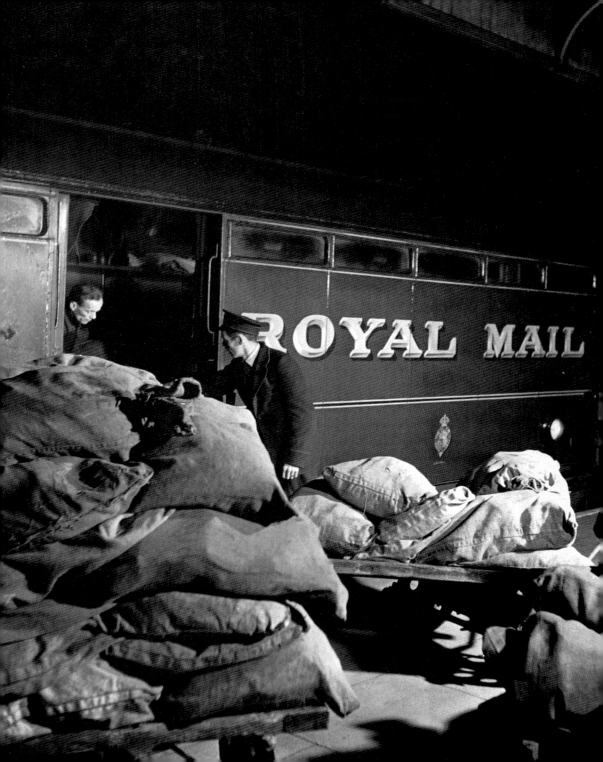

REPORT OF THE POLICE
INVESTIGATION

To HM Chief Inspector of Constabulary, Home Office

On 2nd April 1964 you requested me to prepare a report for the Home Secretary giving details of any lessons which it was thought might be learned by the Police Service as a result of the train robbery which occurred at Cheddington, in Buckinghamshire, on the 8th August 1963 when money to the value of £2,595,997 10s. was stolen.

I have now completed my report and the relevant papers are attached.

My enquiries extended into many fields, both inside and outside the Police Service. At all times I found a complete willingness to render assistance.

The assistance which was rendered to the Buckinghamshire Constabulary by the members of the Metropolitan Police was quite unprecedented. No charge was made to the Buckinghamshire Constabulary by the Commissioner of Police for the services of many of his most experienced specialized officers; a very clear indication of the wonderful cooperation which now exists in the Police Service.

It has been my honest intention to try and avoid 'being wise after the event' and it has also been my intention during the whole of this enquiry to avoid criticizing just for the sake of being critical. I have endeavoured to abstract from the vast volume of information which was available to me the clear lessons which the Police Service as a whole can learn from this case.

It was considered necessary to postpone the final drafting of my report and findings until after the appeals of those convicted of this crime had been settled. It is for this reason that my enquiries have taken a little longer than I at first anticipated.

The detective chief superintendent of the Research and Planning Branch of the Home Office was made available to me to

Fingerprint files at New Scotland Yard, the London headquarters of the Metropolitan Police, 1959 assist in the necessary research work. When the magnitude of the task was fully appreciated, at my request the chief constable of Warwickshire very kindly made a senior officer of that force available for a period of six weeks.

I should like to pay tribute to both these officers for all the help which they have given me.

HMI

6th October 1964

Buckinghamshire Constabulary

The county of Buckinghamshire lies to the north and west of London. The headquarters of the County Constabulary is at Aylesbury which is 40 miles from London. The northern part of the county is rural whilst that in the south, particularly where the county adjoins London, is industrial and heavily populated. Counties immediately surrounding Buckinghamshire are Northamptonshire on the north, Bedfordshire and Hertfordshire on the east, Oxfordshire and Berkshire on the west and Middlesex in the south. The acreage is 479,411 and the population at the time of the robbery was 508,000. There are 1,012 miles of classified roads and 1,024 miles of unclassified roads making a total of 2,036 miles.

Establishment
Police
The authorized establishment of the force on 8th August 1963 was as follows:

1	chief constable
1	assistant chief constable
2	chief superintendents
6	superintendents class 1
7	chief inspectors
38	inspectors
99	sergeants
537	constables
1	woman police inspector
3	women police sergeants
21	women police constables

PROBABLE ROUTE TAKEN BY THE ROBBERS

Buckingham

Milton Keynes

A421

Padbury

A413

Grand Union Canal

A5

Leighton Buzzard

Five miles

Bridego Bridge: Train robbe offloaded the mailbags here, af stopping the travelling post offi near Sears Crossing.

Leaving **Bridego Bridge** about 3.30 a.m. and following mostly 'C' class roads, the robbers probably arrived at **Leatherslade Farm** around 4.30 a.m., just as the first message was being transmitted by Buckinghamshire Police.

Linslade

Cublington

Whitchurch   A413   Wing

Quinton

Oving

A418

Ledburn

A505

Dunstable

Luton

J11

1

A5

Horton

Cheddington station

Bicester

A41

Kingswood

BUCKINGHAMSHIRE

2

Waddesdon

A41

Aylesbury

A418

Brill

3

Oakley

M40

Thame

J9

Wheatley

J8

A40

J7

A329

OXFORDSHIRE

Grand Union Canal

Stoke Mandeville

Haddenham

Ivinghoe

A4146

HERTFORDSHIR

Tring

Hemel Hempstead

A41

Wendover

Berkhamsted

Princes Risborough

A413

Great Missenden

Chesham

A41

Bovingdon

M2

Amersham

LEATHERSLADE FARM

⑤

④

FARMHOUSE

①

②

③

⑦

⑥

B4011

1 Open shed
2 Open shed
3 Garage
4 Derelict shed
5 Garage
6 Cow sheds
7 Dutch barns

GLASGOW

LONDON

Authorized male establishment 691. Actual male establishment on
8th August 1963 was 683.

Civilians

196

Traffic Division

1	superintendent
2	inspectors
9	sergeants
51	constables

TOTAL 63

Vehicles

Traffic cars	13 + 3 relief
Criminal Investigation Department cars	9
Car for officer at C9	1
Ford Anglia training car	1
Austin A60 driving instruction	1
General purpose cars	34
Relief Anglia	1
Morris 1000 Road Safety traveller	1
A55 photography van	1
A55 Utilicon vans	3
Morris Minor stores van	1
5 cwt dog vans	4
Light removal van	1
General purpose busettes	5
Land rover	1
Traffic motor cycles	4
General purpose motor cycles	45
Motor cycles training	2
Motor cycles relief	1

TOTAL 132

Detective superintendent	1
Detective chief inspector	1
Detective inspectors	5
Detective sergeants	13
Detective constables	46
TOTAL	66

On outside duty at the time of the robbery 8th August 1963

The strength of the force on duty for Buckinghamshire as a whole at the time of the robbery at 3.30 a.m. 8th August 1963 was:

3 wireless cars	6 police constables
5 modified team patrol cars	9 police constables
	1 sergeant
Cycle patrol	1 police constable
Dog patrol	1 sergeant
Beat patrols	5 sergeants
	32 constables

MAJOR DISASTERS

A scheme is in existence in Buckinghamshire to be implemented when a major disaster occurs. The local police strength can be augmented by the implementation of a mutual aid plan which shows that 135 police officers of up to and including the rank of chief inspector can be made available at short notice. Within a period of five hours a total number of 260 police officers can be available. In addition, military personnel is also available if required.

THE LINSLADE SUB-DIVISION

With an acreage of 43,600 and a population of 13,000, the Linslade sub-division is situated to the east of Aylesbury. It comprises six police beats under the charge of an inspector assisted by two sergeants and 10 constables. Five of the constables are station-ed on detached beats outside and around Linslade whilst the remaining staff are at Linslade. There is a wireless equipped car for sub-divisional use and four motor cycles without wireless. There are 207 farms and small-holdings on the sub-division and two disused RAF airfields. The main Glasgow–Euston railway line passes through 12 miles of the sub-division, there being a small railway station at Cheddington (one of the detached beat officers' stations). The Cheddington beat has 32 farms and small-holdings as its share of the total mentioned. The four miles of railway line on the beat pass to the east of the village of Cheddington; the rail-way station is a typically small village station which closes down after the last train in the evening until the following morning. The maximum amount of money held at the station booking office overnight is never more than £2–3 and security arrangements existing are adequate to take this into account. There is a court house adjoining the Linslade Police Station where the magistrates sit on alternate Wednesdays.

Following the robbery the local officer from Cheddington was attached to work with the headquarters enquiry team from Ayles-bury and was so engaged until 23rd March 1964. In the first instance his local knowledge of the area was of importance to the investigation and he later settled into the incident room side of the enquiry where he remained.

After the first day, when all the sub-divisional personnel were engaged on enquiries and searching, only the inspector in charge is noted on the duty sheets as booked out to enquiries regarding the robbery; other staff pursued 'normal' detached beat officer type enquiries. The expression 'normal' here is used in the context of mode of enquiry rather than amount, as obviously with a crime of this magnitude in their midst activity would be very much increased. Nevertheless, with the exception of the Cheddington officer, rest days were taken as normal.

Following the discovery of Leatherslade Farm on 13th August 1963, the Linslade sub-division was called upon to supply officers on six consecutive days to a maximum of four constables. On the first two days a sergeant from the sub-division was called upon for duty there. Sixty-eight telephone messages are filed at the sub-divisional office relating to the robbery, not including express messages; four gave instruction on aspects of the robbery in general and there were 64 specific enquiries.

At the time of the committal and trial proceedings, the inspector in charge of Linslade sub-division was placed in charge of the court arrangements working with the chief inspector of Aylesbury. This was spread over a period of months and must have proved an extraordinary burden on the division and sub-division.

THE WADDESDON SECTION

Situated within the Aylesbury Division of the Buckinghamshire force is the Waddesdon section, which comprises approximately 57,500 acres of land to the north-west of Aylesbury. The population of 12,000 reside in 26 villages and other small hamlets within the area. There are 290 farms and small-holdings on the section and a number of disused Army and RAF campsites are scattered over it.

Policing is carried out by a sergeant at section headquarters (Waddesdon) and eight constables. The sergeant is directly responsible to the sub-divisional inspectors who work from Aylesbury. Five of the constables are stationed on detached beats, four of whom are equipped with motor cycles (no wireless); other transport for the section comprises a wireless-equipped section car (shared with Aylesbury but garaged at Waddesdon) and a further motor cycle at section headquarters. Duties for the section are

arranged by the sergeant whose own duties are always discretionary, having regard to his overall 24-hour responsibility for the section and its officers.

Following information of the robbery on 8th August 1963, the two constables on duty at Waddesdon Police Station assisted the sergeant with a road check principally on the A413 at Whitchurch. Spot checks as mentioned in the first message to the force were also carried out. A search was made of a disused aerodrome and an ex-ammunition dump on the section, and detached beat officers contacted some of the farmers in the area asking them to report anything suspicious. Rest days continued as normal up until the discovery of Leatherslade Farm, which aspect of the robbery is dealt with separately and in detail later in the report.

With the exception of the constable responsible for the Brill beat, whose duties and activities are covered later, the section was not called upon to supply personnel for the Brill incident post when it was functioning, but was quite heavily committed in supplying officers for guard duty – three out of four available one day; three out of three on another. Specific enquiries concerning the robbery were dealt with through the headquarters incident room and sent out from there for enquiry by local officers where appropriate. This did not involve the section in any unduly high proportion of work.

One of the out-station constables mentioned is at Brill, which has a population of 900. It was formerly a market town, but today it is mainly a farming community. Motor-cycle scrambles are held there in which the owner of Leatherslade Farm prior to the train robbery played a leading part. Brill is 600 feet above sea level and has a commanding view of the surrounding countryside. Until the outbreak of war it was an inspectors' station; a magistrates' court sits there on the fourth Monday of each month, in a court room adjoining the police station.

For a time from 1957 a sergeant and two constables were stationed there; this was later reduced to two constables until late in 1962 when the station became that for one man only.

The beat itself has five parishes, Brill, Oakley, Boarstill, Worminghall and Dorton. It covers 12,000 acres and has a total population approaching 2,500. Very little crime is reported on this beat – 9 in 1963 – although this had in its make-up a case originally reported as murder. All in all it is a fairly typical country beat officers' station with all its attendant problems of traffic, diseases of animals and so on. There are 52 farms and small-holdings on the beat.

The train and the attack

The attacked train was known as the Glasgow to Euston Travelling Post Office. It was and still is sometimes referred to as the 'Up' Special or the 'Up' Postal. It was a night train and part of it left Glasgow at 6.50 p.m. 7th August 1963. It stopped first at Carstairs (28 miles south of Glasgow), where other coaches were added to it, and also at Carlisle where further coaches were added making the complete train. The train consisted solely of an engine manned by a railway engine driver and fireman and a number of coaches in which GPO employees were engaged in sorting mail. A railway guard was positioned in a section at the rear of the last coach. There were no passenger coaches or railway freight carrying coaches attached to the train. The train was scheduled to arrive at Euston at 3.59 a.m. 8th August 1963.

The robbery took place on the night run of 7th/8th August 1963, at a section between Sears Crossing signal gantry and Bridego Bridge in the parish of Mentmore in the county of Buckinghamshire, a distance of roughly two miles from Leighton Buzzard and about 38 miles from Euston. The time of commencement of this offence can firmly be established at 3.03 a.m. 8th August 1963, but the time taken to complete the offence and steal the property can only be assessed from witnesses as being in the region of half an hour.

The property stolen consisted of 120 mailsacks, each containing one or more mailbags which in turn held 636 high-valued packets, to the total value of £2,595,997 10s. A high-valued packet is one that is registered and posted by a bank.

The travelling post office at the time of the attack consisted of a diesel engine and 12 coaches. It will be seen that the coaches, in

SEARS CROS

SLOW IB TELEPHONE

UP SLOW LINE

LEIGHTON BUZZARD Nº I

SIG. 12

addition to being numbered, are marked DG, POS, or POT. A reference to these marks is shown on the plan but for information it should be mentioned here that the coaches marked BG, and POT, were being used only to transport mail, whilst those marked POS were actually being used as sorting offices and it was in those coaches that the Post Office employees were engaged.

A corridor ran along the train from the rear coach to the second coach. The corridor terminated there because the communicating doorway between the first and the second coaches was offset. The first coach, therefore, had no communication either with the remainder of the train or with the diesel engine.

The coach marked POS 30204 was known as the HVP coach, that is the one carrying high-valued packets. All the packets in this coach originated from banks and were being transported to the East Central District Post Office, London, for delivery to the head offices of the various banks concerned. Sorting of bags containing these packets into mailbags and sacks was being carried out by GPO staff. None of the other coaches contained high-valued packets.

Altogether on the train sorting mail were 77 Post Office employees. They were under the direction and control of a Post Office inspector and an assistant inspector. In charge of the HVP coach was a higher-grade postman and at the time of the robbery he was in that coach with the assistant inspector and three other higher-grade postmen. The inspector was in the fifth coach and the other postmen working were scattered through various coaches of the train.

Usually, travelling post office trains are kept running to schedule, and it is unusual for delays. They of course have to obey the normal traffic signals. Without going into too much detail, it is sufficient to say that there are two signals to each section of track. These are known as the distant and home signals. The distant signal is the first signal seen by the driver and consists of two lights,

DIESEL LOCOMOTIVE

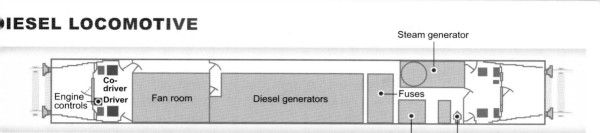

Steam generator

Co-driver

Driver

Engine controls

Fan room

Diesel generators

Fuses

Battery container   Toilet

SORTING VAN

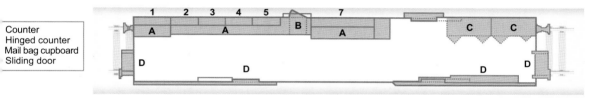

Counter
Hinged counter
Mail bag cupboard
Sliding door

1 2 3 4 5 B 7 A C C

A

A

D   D   D   D

PLAN OF ROYAL MAIL TRAIN UNIT

DIESEL LOCOMOTIVE   PARCEL VAN   SORTING VAN

one amber and one green. If the amber light is showing it is a cautionary signal to the engine driver that he is likely to find the home signal at danger and he should, therefore, apply his brakes. The home signal also consists of two lights, one red and one green. If the red light is showing the engine must stop. These signals are controlled by a signal box, although an automatic device is included in the system so that when any signal is passed by a train at green it automatically reverts to either 'caution' or 'stop' (according to what type of signal it is) until the train has passed out of the section controlled by it. At each home signal is placed a telephone with calling facilities to the signal box controlling the section. The reason for this is that should a train be delayed more than three minutes it is the duty of the fireman to telephone the signal box to find out the reason for delay and thereby check the possibility of a signal fault.

Having set out the information respecting the train which helps in understanding the case, it is now proposed to deal with it in more detail.

The travelling post office is a composite train built up of coaches collected on its journey to Euston. The engine and first five coaches left Glasgow at 6.50 p.m. on 7th August 1963, arriving at Carstairs at 7.32 p.m. There it is joined by four more coaches which left Aberdeen at 3.30 p.m. on 7th August 1963, and arrived at Carstairs at 7.15 p.m. These coaches were attached to the rear of the Glasgow train and, therefore, formed a section of it, consisting of coaches six to nine. The engine and nine coaches then left Carstairs at 7.45 p.m. arriving at Carlisle at 8.54 p.m. There three further coaches were added to the train. These again were attached to the rear of the train and therefore formed that section of it consisting of coaches ten to twelve.

At Carlisle the original guard on the train was relieved, and his replacement took up his duties as guard from that moment and was with the train until it was attacked.

The train left Carlisle at 9.04 p.m. and stopped at Preston from 10.53 p.m. to 11.03 p.m., Warrington from 11.36 p.m. to 11.43 p.m. and Crewe from 12.12 a.m. the 8th August 1963 to 12.30 a.m. At Crewe the original driver and fireman of the train were relieved, and their replacements then drove the train on the remainder of the journey, stopping at Tamworth from 1.23 a.m. to 1.30 a.m. and at Rugby from 2.12 a.m. to 2.17 a.m., finally passing Bletchley at 2.53 a.m. The journey continued until finally at 3.03 a.m. the train stopped just before Sears Crossing home signal because it showed red against it. It was there that the robbery took place.

At this stage, a description of the robbery is omitted until the boarding places and movements of essential witnesses, employed by the GPO and engaged on the train, have been shown. An inspector was in charge of the travelling post office from Carlisle to Euston. His operational position in the train was in the fifth coach back from the engine. During the journey he did patrol the train but at the time of the robbery was at his operational position.

It is now proposed to deal with the five Post Office employees who were in the high-valued packets coach at the time of the robbery. An assistant inspector was in charge of the train from Carlisle to Euston. His main duty was to supervise the staff in the second to fourth coaches behind the engine. A postman higher grade was in charge of the high-valued packets coach from Carlisle to Euston. A further postman higher grade was also employed in the high-valued packets coach from Carlisle to Euston. The third postman higher grade joined the train at Tamworth at about 1.30 a.m. on 8th August 1963. He was employed in the fifth coach from the engine until just before 3.00 a.m. when he was instructed by the inspector to report to the high-valued packets coach. The fourth postman higher grade joined the train at Tamworth at about 1.30 a.m.

and was employed throughout the train sorting mail. Just a few minutes before the robbery he was also instructed to report to the high-valued packets coach for duty.

The stretch of railroad on which this offence occurred consists of four sets of tracks. The train was travelling on the 'Up' fast line, travelling from north to south. As the engine approached the distant signal, which is a dwarf one and is situated 1,300 yards before the home signal at Sears Crossing, the driver saw the light was at 'caution'. He immediately began to apply his brakes. He then noticed that the home signal was at red, so he brought his train to a standstill about five or six yards in front of the signal gantry. He was sitting in the driver's seat, which is on the left side of the engine facing forward. The fireman immediately left his seat on the right, passed behind the driver and climbed down on to the tracks. He went to the telephone which is below the signal and between the second and third sets of lines. It will be remembered that earlier in the report it was shown that the railway instruction was on finding a signal at 'stop' to delay for three minutes before telephoning. However, the fireman's promptness on this occasion was not unusual because apparently this person never waits the regulation time. From where he was on the tracks the fireman could see the distant signal for the next section of line at green, which was an indication that the line ahead was clear and their stop light a fault.

The fireman, on getting to the telephone, tried to contact the signal box at Leighton Buzzard but was unable to get any reply. He noticed that the wires to the telephone had been cut. From this point onwards there appears to have been some confusion between the driver and the fireman, but generally speaking their story is consistent.

After noticing the telephone wires were cut, the fireman says that he saw a man looking in between the second and third coaches and thinking he was a postman from the train he went towards him. As he passed the engine he said to the driver 'I'll go and see what's wrong.' He went up to the man and said 'What's wrong mate?' The man did not appear to hear him and walked away towards the left-hand embankment, that is the east embankment, saying as he did so 'Come here', and at the same time he beckoned with his hand. The fireman followed him, thinking by this time that he was a railway man and that he was going to tell him what was wrong. The reason for his change of mind regarding the man's employment was because he noticed when he got up to him at the coach that he was wearing what is known by railwaymen as a 'slop', that is a bib-and-brace overall with a jacket on top. This is usually worn by firemen and drivers.

The fireman followed the man to the top of the railway embankment where he was grabbed by the elbows and pushed down the embankment. It was then that he noticed two other men lying below him. As he stumbled and slid down the embankment one of the men grabbed him, put his hand over his mouth, a cosh under his nose and said, 'If you shout I'll kill you.' The fireman openly admits he was terrified and said to the man 'All right mate, I am on your side.'

By this time the other two men had gone out of the fireman's view and he presumed they had gone to the engine. Eventually he was told to get up and he was walked towards the engine. As he climbed into the cab he saw five or six men in it. Someone turned him bodily to face the back wall of the cab. He was told to put his arms behind his back and he felt someone fumbling with his left wrist and then he was pushed into the passage of the engine room. There he saw the driver with his head covered in blood and a man standing behind him who was holding a cosh. This man told the fireman to close his eyes and keep them closed.

A few moments later the driver was taken to the driving cab and

a little later the fireman felt the train on the move. He remained in the passageway with his face towards one of the walls until he felt the train stop, and then, after a few moments, the driver was brought back into the passageway and they were handcuffed together. Both of them were then made to get down on the tracks and their escort led them to the right (or west) embankment and made them lie down on their stomachs with their faces to the ground. The fireman did see to the south of him on the same embankment what appeared to be a piece of white rag stretched between sticks and which he believed to be a marker placed there by the thieves. This was later taken possession of by the police and was obviously a sign used by the thieves to stop the train after they had taken control and possession of it.

Within a few minutes both the driver and the fireman were made to stand up and they were led to the rear end of the train. It was then that the fireman discovered that only two coaches (the first two) were coupled to the engine. They were again instructed to close their eyes but the fireman did not do so and he saw that the train was stopped on a bridge over a roadway (Bridego Bridge). He noticed parked near the bridge what appeared to him to be an army lorry of three to five tons. (When first interviewed he thought it was a 10-ton lorry but then reconsidered his opinion.) He also saw a mailsack which fell at his feet on the rail track. They were taken to a position just north of the end of the train and made to sit on the railway embankment. After a couple of minutes they were made to stand up and were taken to the rear of the second coach and ordered to enter. They did this with difficulty, bearing in mind that they were handcuffed together, and with the help of their escort. The fireman noticed as he got into the coach that the postal workers were lying on their faces at the far end of it. They were ordered by their escort not to move for half an hour and indirectly threatened that if they did they would be hurt. The

In the cab of a steam train

escort then left them and all the occupants of the coach obeyed his instruction.

The fireman estimates that it was about half an hour later that the guard of the train came to the coach. He was told what had happened and he went away for assistance. A parcels train travelling on the 'Up' slow line stopped and the fireman of that train, having been told what had happened, drove the engine and two coaches of the travelling post office into Cheddington Railway Station. They were later seen by police and an ambulance took the fireman and driver to hospital. The former was uninjured but as the driver was handcuffed to him and was injured, both had to go to the hospital.

As previously stated, the driver's recollection of the events generally confirmed those of the fireman, although there were understandable differences which undoubtedly can be accounted for by the suddenness of the attack and the injuries received by him. These differences and additions will now be brought out.

The driver says that after the fireman had attempted to telephone the signal box he returned to the foot of the cabin, told him that the telephone wires had been cut and then walked away towards the back of the engine. The driver turned his head to follow his movements and saw two men coming from the embankment (bottom or east side of tracks) whom he took to be linesmen dealing with the signal failure. Assuming this to be the case, the driver turned to his control, released his brake lever and began to build up the necessary pressure needed to release the brakes, expecting to be told to proceed. He did not see the man looking between the coaches and thought the fireman was going back to talk to the two men he had seen coming from the embankment.

Having dealt with his controls, the driver turned to his left expecting to see the fireman returning. He was surprised by another man who had climbed up on to the footplate and who was holding a cosh in his hand ready to strike him. He grabbed at this man and almost forced him from the footplate but was struck from behind by someone who must have entered the cab from the other side. The driver fell to the floor, stunned, and the next thing he remembers was the cab apparently full of men and he heard someone say 'Don't look up or you'll get some more.' Understandably he was frightened and from then on did as he was told. He was instructed to get up, keep his head bent down and go into the engine-room passage. He was pushed in and there saw his colleague with a masked man. This is a reversal of what the fireman said as he claims he went into the passageway and saw the driver there and a man with a cosh.

About 30 seconds later the driver was pulled out of the passageway, made to take his driving seat, keep his head bent down and to drive the train. As he opened the controller of the diesel engine and began to move off he realized he was not getting full vacuum pressure and so he opened the large ejector in order to clear completely the air from the vacuum pipes and thus fully release the brakes. He says that the necessity for taking this action suggested to him that a coach had been uncoupled and that the disconnected vacuum pipe had been returned but the stopper had not been fixed properly. He drove the train for what he estimates as half a mile. This estimate was on movement and not what he saw. It is known now that the actual distance was about 1,200 yards. He was told to stop and did so by applying the brakes fully; he was then led back into the passage where he was handcuffed to the fireman.

The driver's story then follows roughly the same pattern as that given by the fireman except that the driver saw about 10 men unloading mailbags from the coach in chain fashion. When he was lying on the ground he saw the thieves passing the mailbags down the embankment.

The fireman was only able to describe one man, that was the man he first saw at the railway coach. This man was the only man he can definitely say was unmasked. His general impression was that the men were wearing boiler suits and balaclava helmets. He attended photo albums at the Criminal Record Office in New Scotland Yard on the 13th August 1963, but was unable to identify anyone. The driver was only able to say that all the men were wearing boiler suits and balaclava helmets.

Dealing with the Post Office employees previously mentioned, the inspector was on duty in the fifth coach and his story does not assist.

The assistant inspector who was in the high-valued packets coach with the four postmen higher grade says that the train stopped between Leighton Buzzard and Cheddington and he estimates the time at 3.15 a.m. This time is incorrect as will be seen later. A few minutes later the train began to move and he heard steam escaping from the rear of his coach and he formed the opinion that the coupling between his coach and the next had broken. Someone pulled the communication cord and others shouted through the windows to attract the attention of the driver. No further action could be taken by them to draw the driver's attention to the position because there was no corridor communication between the high-valued packets coach and the parcels van which separates the former from the diesel engine.

The assistant inspector said that in accordance with instructions all doors and windows of the high-valued packets coach were closed and fastened. (This was untrue because the corridor door of the HVP coach was only capable of being locked by a spigot key and there was no indication that this key was turned. A hook and ring higher on the door were not capable of being fastened.) The train travelled for what he estimated to be half a mile and then stopped again. A window of the coach was broken. He

The train robbers lugged the sacks from the train to their army-type truck
(parked where second car is seen).

shouted to the others that it was a raid and they all began piling mailbags against the sliding doors as a barricade and the other doors were bolted. Someone outside shouted 'They are barricading the doors. Get the guns.' Another window was broken and two men climbed through it into the coach waving coshes. Other men entered through the rear gangway door and one of them was waving an axe. Within seconds the assistant inspector says six to eight unauthorized men were in the coach and he could hear others shouting outside. One of the men hit him on the arm with a cosh and then all the GPO men were herded into the front of the coach and made to lie down. The man with the cosh stood guard over them making them keep their heads down and eyes closed.

The assistant inspector heard the sound of mailbags being unloaded. Afterwards they were told not to leave the coach for half an hour. He saw the driver and fireman come into the back of the coach. He noticed the driver was injured. As soon as things appeared quiet he and one of the postmen higher grade left the attacked coach and walked back along the tracks to the remainder of the train. On the way he says he met the guard and told him what had happened. The other Post Office men on the coach, broadly speaking, support this evidence. There are, however, differences of opinion as to the exact sequence of events and what part each played in trying to protect themselves or the coach. No doubt their differences are the result of fear which was put into them when mention of guns was made by one of the raiders. None of these Post Office men could identify any of their attackers. Composite descriptions of two of the men were made. Each was wearing a stocking or a balaclava over his face.

In the third coach of the train, that is the coach immediately behind the high-valued packets coach, were four other Post Office employees. Two of them were higher-grade postmen.

One joined the train at Carlisle and was present in his coach when the train stopped at Sears Crossing. After it had been stationary for a few minutes, out of curiosity, he opened the nearside door of his coach and saw a man standing between his coach and the high-valued packets coach. After a few seconds he saw another man come from under and beneath the joining bellows of the two coaches. One of them spoke to the other and they then both walked away towards the diesel engine. He thought no more of this because he believed the two men to be railwaymen who had effected a repair. He closed the door and walked through his coach towards the bellows of the high-valued packets coach and as he did so he saw it move away and suddenly the steam pipe burst and his vision was impaired due to escaping steam. When the steam cleared he saw that the high-valued packets coach was drawing further away and one of the GPO employees inside it was closing the corridor door. He still did not realize anything was seriously wrong, but he was puzzled because he noticed the signal at red.

He gave a description of the first man and said he was wearing a railwayman's cap but not shiny-topped, and blue material-type clothing similar to that worn by railwaymen. He was not wearing a mask. The second man was dressed similarly and he cannot say whether he was wearing a mask as he did not see his face. He attended photo albums at New Scotland Yard but failed to make any identification.

The second postman higher grade joined the train at Crewe and was in the same coach as his colleague when the train stopped at Sears Crossing. He looked out of the sliding door in the coach and in the darkness could just make out two figures standing at the side of the track near the couplings between his coach and the high-valued packets coach. He later saw the engine and first two coaches go off down the track on their own. He cannot recognize either man.

The guard was in his compartment at the rear of the train when it

stopped at Sears Crossing. He recorded the time as 3.03 a.m. Two minutes later he heard the brakes go on and saw the vacuum gauge in his department drop to zero. He walked through to the ninth coach, spoke to the GPO inspector (who, after the train stopped, walked through the train from the fifth coach and had reached the ninth), and then got down on to the nearside track. He looked towards where the diesel engine should have been but could not see it. Neither did he see anyone. He walked towards the front of the train expecting to meet the fireman. He continued the length of the train and found the engine and first two coaches missing. He could not hear the diesel engine or see any sign of it. He returned to the ninth coach and asked the GPO staff in it to apply the handbrake. He then returned to his compartment, collected detonators and walked away from the train back towards Leighton Buzzard, laying detonators on the track at a quarter of a mile, half a mile and one mile from the train. He then returned to Sears Crossing signals where he found the signal box telephone wires had been cut. He continued along the line believing something serious had happened but not realizing that the train had been robbed. He placed detonators at 100 yards from the train and then decided to walk to Cheddington. He came across the remainder of the train at Bridego Bridge.

The guard noticed the nearside door of the high-valued packets coach open and also the corridor door. Inside the coach he saw the driver and the fireman sitting on some bags handcuffed together. He noticed the injuries to the driver. He also saw three of the GPO staff inside the coach. They told him of the robbery and he then set off towards Cheddington Station to seek assistance. He stopped a train which was coming towards him, told the guard of the robbery and asked him to stop at the abandoned diesel engine and attend to it. He then continued to walk towards Cheddington and en route was picked up by a passing train. At Cheddington signal box he arranged for assistance. He recorded his time of arrival there as 4.15 a.m.

The scene of the robbery: the train waiting on an embankment above a country road

The two men who the guard did not see in the coach were the assistant inspector and one of the postmen higher grade. They had left the high-valued packets coach and walked along the line to the other nine coaches. They were under the impression that they had passed the guard and told him what had happened. The guard denied this, but agreed that he saw only three GPO men in the high-valued packets coach when he arrived there. Other GPO employees in that coach confirm that one or more of their numbers did leave the coach before the guard arrived. Subsequent enquiries showed that the two men had spoken, not to Miller but to the fireman of a parcels train who had been instructed to watch out for the travelling post office.

The signalman on duty at Leighton Buzzard No. 1 signal box during the night of 7th/8th August 1963 saw the travelling post office pass his signal box at 2.58 a.m. At 3 a.m. he received an indication on a buzzer in his box that the signal lights at the distant signal at Sears Crossing were out. He assumed it was a signal failure and took no action but waited for a telephone call from the fireman on the travelling post office. He did not receive such a call and at 3.10 a.m. the signalman from Cheddington signal box telephoned him to enquire where the train was. He told him that the train had entered his section and of the signal failure. At 3.15 a.m. the signalman noticed on his indicator that the train had passed the signals at Sears Crossing. At the same time his indicator showed the approach line to Sears Crossing as being still engaged. He assumed that a vehicle or part of the train had been left behind or that there was a track failure. He arranged for a linesman to be called out to check the line and advised the Control Office, Euston, and the signalman at Cheddington box of the circumstances and of his intention to ask the driver of the next 'Up' train to examine the line and report the position of the travelling post office at Cheddington. He later spoke to the driver

Engineer moving the robbed train into Cheddington station for police inspection. It was from these controls that the driver was slugged after being forced to drive the train further along the line.

of the next 'Up' train, who, as a result of this action, discovered the travelling post office and was informed of the robbery. He instructed his fireman to take the front position of the travelling post office to Cheddington. On the way to Cheddington this driver spoke to Euston Control and asked them to arrange for the police and ambulance to attend.

A technician of the Signal and Telecommunications Department of British Railways arrived at 4.45 a.m. at Sears Crossing. He found that all four signal box telephone wires had been cut and that the home signal had been interfered with. He examined it and saw four dry cell batteries connected by wires to the red bulb with a switch in between. The green light was covered by a man's glove. This would have the effect of preventing any lights showing on the signal until the switch was thrown, when a red light would appear. When he examined the signal the red light was showing.

An assistant linesman arrived at Sears Crossing at 5.10 a.m. and assisted in repairing the telephone wires. He then examined the distant signal and found the bulb missing from the green aspect. He also found an electric lead with two crocodile clips attached hanging over the door of the signal. He saw that the lead went across one set of rails and that where it lay on the rails it had been cut, obviously by a passing train. In the track itself he found two further lengths of wire and on one of these was a brown 'on' and 'off' switch; but he did not find any batteries. His conclusion was that the same principle had been adopted to cause a 'cautionary' signal on the distant signal as had been adopted to cause a stop signal on the home signal. The only difference was that instead of using a glove to obliterate the green light the bulb had been removed from the green aspect.

The Joint British Railways Board, London Midland Region, held an inquiry at Euston on 12th August 1963 into the circumstances of the stopping and robbery of the train. This is referred to later in the report.

The driver of the travelling post office was taken to the Royal Bucks Hospital, Aylesbury, where he was examined and treated by the senior house surgeon. He was found to have a number of lacerations to the head and 14 stitches were inserted. He was detained for observation and treatment and was discharged on 10th August 1963. He did not work again for some considerable time but at the time of writing this report he has now started light duties. The clothing he was wearing at the time of the attack was not taken possession of at Aylesbury but was recovered for scientific examination from his home in Crewe on the 12th August 1963. A blood sample was also taken from the driver on this date at the Barony Hospital, Nantwich.

The escape by the thieves from the scene to Leatherslade Farm

Having described the attacks and the robbery, it is obvious, from choice of position and the cutting of telephone wires, that the thieves were successful in delaying information of the robbery coming to the notice of the police. From the time the train was first brought to a halt at Sears Crossing at 3.03 a.m. and the thieves leaving Bridego Bridge at about 3.30 a.m., it was not until 4.25 a.m. that a telephone call from Cheddington signal box reached Aylesbury, via Euston and New Scotland Yard. This message and others are dealt with later. The first police car containing two police officers is recorded as arriving at Cheddington at 4.36 a.m.

The probable route taken by the thieves from Cheddington to Leatherslade Farm is one which is reconstructed from information given by witnesses and can be described as follows:

It winds its way over almost wholly 'C' class roads and through completely rural countryside. Three points on the route cross over 'A' class roads which presumably the thieves would regard as danger points in their escape. Had the information of the robbery to the police been immediate, however, these points would not have been manned as nowhere do they appear on the No. 5 District Check-point Scheme. By their very nature, they are not points which would attract immediate attention as being likely interception points, unless there had been early information of the likely route the thieves were taking. In this case there was no such information.

Leaving Bridego Bridge one travels westwards following 'C' roads Nos 49 and 37 through Ledburn via C75 and 76 to Wing, when in a straight-ahead movement the A418 Aylesbury to Leighton Buzzard road is crossed; then via C8 and 71 to

Cublington and Whitchurch where the A413 is crossed in a movement which involves travelling the 'A' class road for approximately 300 yards. The C57 via Oving and Pitchcott takes one to Quainton and Kingswood by C25, 30, 75 and 112, where the A41 is crossed in a straight-ahead movement. The C3 and C60 then take one to Brill and on to the B4011 Thame road where, after turning left, the Leatherslade Farm entrance is within 400 yards.

This whole route takes a vehicle from the scene via a completely rural route to the north of Aylesbury and from the east to the west side of the county. (Cheddington is close to the Hertfordshire border and Brill to the Oxfordshire border.)

It is known the thieves were using two land rovers and a 5-ton motor lorry and travelling in convoy. Information has it that the thieves had a transistor radio on which they heard the first message transmitted by Buckinghamshire Police which was at 4.28 a.m. on 8th August 1963. At this time they were just turning into Leatherslade Farm. Although there is no evidence to support this information, if correct, it means that the thieves took about one hour for the journey. The route over which the thieves travelled was measured and found to be 28 miles (17 miles as the crow flies between point of attack and Leatherslade). Going over the route in daylight by motorcar travelling at speeds between 35/40 miles per hour the journey took 48 minutes.

THE CUTTING OF GPO TELEPHONE LINES

During the early period of the inquiry it came to notice that between certain times on 7th and 8th August 1963 telephone wires to four private houses in the area of the robbery were cut. The Post Office engineer who examined and repaired the wires went to Bridego Bridge, Mentmore, at about 5.30 p.m. on 8th August 1963.

He examined a telegraph pole and found that four wires had been cut about 12 inches away from the insulator fixed to the pole.

He repaired the breaks and then checked the telephones Leighton Buzzard 46724 and 69714 and found them to be working correctly. At about 6.30 p.m. the same day he went to a farm in Slapton. He examined a telephone pole and found that the wires had been cut on both sides of it about 12 inches from the insulator. He also noticed that grass surrounding the pole had been trampled down and bruised. He repaired the breaks and then checked the telephones Leighton Buzzard 69824 and 63382 and found them to be working correctly. The engineer had at 2.45 a.m. on 8th August 1963 repaired a fault at the Leighton Buzzard telephone exchange. At the time he did not attach any importance to it, but when later he repaired the telephone wires at Slapton he realized that the cutting of them was probably responsible for the fault.

It is of interest to note from the statements of the four subscribers who were most affected that the latest time that one of these telephones can be said to be in order on 7th August 1963 was 10.30 p.m. The engineer's statement, however, suggests that the likely time that the telephones were put out of order was about 2.30 a.m. on the 8th August 1963, which was just over half an hour before the robbery took place.

It can be said generally that the thieves had taken a great deal of trouble to ensure that the occupants remaining on the train, split as it was into two sections, were cut off from immediate contact with the outside world so far as was possible. Even presuming that the staff knew precisely where they were at that time and had not been in a state of extreme fear and anxiety it would have needed at least 20 minutes to reach a point where contact could be made to obtain assistance. It will be remembered that when the train was halted the fireman discovered that telephone wires at the signal gantry had been cut on both sides of the line. If these had not been cut, contact would have been made with the section signal box, known as Leighton Buzzard No. 1.

Investigators examine the Royal Mail train involved in the robbery.

Reporting of the crime

The first report to the police of the incident was to the information room, New Scotland Yard, at 4.24 a.m. It was a message from the Control Office, Euston Railway Station, who had received a call from the Cheddington signal box requesting the attendance of police and an ambulance to a break-in at Cheddington Station. This request was relayed at 4.25 a.m. to Buckinghamshire Constabulary headquarters, Aylesbury, and from their information room to two local cars instructing them to attend the scene at once (HB3 Aylesbury divisional car and HB5 Aylesbury traffic car). At 4.28 a.m. HB4 (Bletchley traffic car) was also instructed to attend. At 4.41 a.m. there is a record of the two HB5 police constables being at the scene as brief particulars of the robbery were passed to Aylesbury force headquarters control room. The crew of HB5 say they arrived at the scene at 4.35 a.m.

Contact was also made with the Aylesbury Division, where in accordance with force practice such detail as was then known was telephoned to Linslade Sub-Divisional Police Station. As a rural sub-division the station is not manned for 24 hours and the telephone was switched through to a sergeant's house. The local officer at Cheddington was similarly informed from Aylesbury divisional headquarters and he went at once to the railway station.

The railway station at Cheddington is of fairly recent construction but is small, situated in a rural area and closes down after the last train, shortly after 10 p.m. Only a very small amount of money (£2 to £3) is kept on the premises and a break-in offence there would not create the impression of a particularly serious offence, certainly not of the moment that events disclosed. Suffice it to say, therefore, that the action taken in the first few minutes of the initial report of a crime was adequate having regard to the information then to hand.

Shortly after the attack four GPO staff, from that half of the train which had been left at Sears Crossing, set off in different directions to establish their position and to send for help. One of them found a farm which is not on the telephone; he was however able to rouse the occupier and borrow a bicycle which he used to cycle to Linslade Police Station, a distance of approximately three miles. In the meantime the alarm had already been raised from Cheddington Railway Station, through the Railway Control Room at Euston.

At 4.36 a.m., following the arrival of the motor patrol crew at Cheddington, and within a moment or so the local officers, there was a dramatic change as the true position became known. At almost precisely this time the Linslade sergeant had arrived at the police station, had got out the wireless car HB31, when the GPO man cycled up and his version to the sergeant brought out the sub-divisional inspector, who lives at the police station. This officer was the first to arrive at Sears Crossing, and to make contact with the rear portion of the train. It was within a few minutes of this (5.08 a.m.) that he reported by radio to Aylesbury the serious nature of the crime and asked for every possible assistance. To put it in his own words he said 'Turn the lot out', which was meant to imply the chief constable and other senior officers, particularly the Criminal Investigation Department.

In the meantime the crew of HB5, after first rendering first aid to the driver of the travelling post office and getting as much information as possible, reported back to the control room at Aylesbury by wireless at 4.41 a.m. Two further messages were received at New Scotland Yard from Euston at 4.35 a.m. and 5.08 a.m. respectively. By this time the true position at Cheddington was known at Aylesbury.

The two constables remained at Cheddington Station, on their own initiative, with their car until 8.00 a.m. acting as an incident post. At no time did anyone give them any indication as to the extent of the value of monies stolen. The first they knew as to the extent was when they read it in the evening paper on that day.

Members of London's Metropolitan Police manning switchboard in information room at New Scotland Yard where all 999 calls are received, c.1956

Action taken in Buckinghamshire Constabulary information room

The information room staff consists of:

   (a) Inspector in charge 1

        Sergeants   4

        Constables   8

        Civilians – male   4

The staff is divided into four sections of:

   (b) Sergeants   1

        Constables   2

        Civilians   1

They work a rota of three shifts, namely:

   (c) 10 p.m. to 6 a.m.

        6 a.m. to 2 p.m.

        2 p.m. to 10 p.m.

During the day, there are two female telephonists and one female clerk. On the night of the robbery there was a full staff of one sergeant, two constables and one male civilian on duty.

The first intimation of the robbery was received by telephone from New Scotland Yard at 4.25 a.m. This message was not recorded, but in the control room log it will be seen that Aylesbury traffic car HB5 and Aylesbury divisional car HB3 were instructed to go to Cheddington Railway Station. The Bletchley Division traffic car HB4 was directed to Bletchley Railway Station in case there was some connection between the incident at Cheddington and a train travelling north which might stop at Bletchley.

As the incident was close to the borders of Hertfordshire and Bedfordshire they were contacted by telephone. It was arranged that Bedfordshire would monitor Buckinghamshire broadcasts in case of any development. Aylesbury Division was asked to inform Linslade sub-division and the Cheddington constable, and the Aylesbury dog section was instructed to attend.

At 4.35 a.m., when the true position became known, other officers and wireless vehicles in the county were called out and despatched. Only the log was kept in the information room and this refers to various vehicles by number and the part they played.

The detective superintendent arrived at force headquarters at about 4.50 a.m. and the assistant chief constable at 5.30 a.m. In addition, the inspector in charge of the information room arrived there shortly before 5.30 a.m.

At the time the inspector arrived, one of the police constables in the information room had been sent to the Royal Buckinghamshire Hospital with a handcuff key as it was thought this may assist in releasing the driver and fireman of the train who were handcuffed together. He had been sent on the instructions of the detective superintendent.

The assistant chief constable and the detective superintendent left for the scene about 5.30 a.m. They are shown as being on the way to Cheddington Railway Station at 6.06 a.m. and arriving at Cheddington at 6.17 a.m.

A member of the Buckinghamshire Headquarters Photography and Fingerprint Branch and a detective sergeant of the Aylesbury Division (the detective inspector was on annual leave) were also instructed to attend.

No official telephone messages were made out as it was as much as the staff could do to keep abreast of events. The information room log terminated at 7.06 p.m. 8th August 1963. The set-up of the special incident room to deal with the train robbery will be dealt with later.

ROADBLOCKS

Both the inspector in charge of the information room and his sergeant have mentioned that immediately following the report of the robbery roadblocks were set up. Most information room records concerning actual checks made have been destroyed, and in the Buckinghamshire Constabulary information room, although the points manned are said to have been projected on to a map for the inspection of the assistant chief constable and the detective superintendent, there is no record of these. Enquiries made to find out who did precisely what in this aspect have been inconclusive. As to when checks were cancelled and on whose authority has also been difficult to pinpoint. Some car crews, mainly the two car crews on modified team patrol from the Chesham Division, of their own initiative set up checks they considered likely in their district and left off when their tour of duty was completed. This is indicative of the rather loose overall control in the early stages. It is obvious, however, that no part of the No. 5 District Checkpoints Scheme was put into operation. It must be remembered here, however, that the thieves had left the scene about one hour before the police were informed.

The neighbouring forces of Hertfordshire and Bedfordshire made some road checks following the information received by them at 4.45 a.m. (by telephone) and 4.38 a.m. (wireless monitor) respectively. Oxfordshire, for example, received no information of the crime at this time.

Police investigating the coupling of the carriage

The action at the scene

The scene in its widest sense covers some four miles of railway line. The motor patrol crew of HB5 arrived at Cheddington Railway Station at 4.36 a.m. and were the first to make contact with some of the railway and GPO personnel involved. As mentioned earlier it was a Linslade inspector who first made contact with the rear portion of the train at Redborough Farm Bridge.

This inspector appears to have quickly appreciated the position and was soon aware that a considerable amount of money had been stolen, which fact he says he communicated to the Buckinghamshire Constabulary information room. Following up the line from Redborough he came across the train proper and HVP coach. He noted various exhibits along the line and their position for later reference to the Criminal Investigation Department. In passing his messages to force headquarters he asked, in addition to senior officers' attendance, for roadblocks to be set up around the area, for neighbouring police stations to be informed and patrols to operate adjacent to the area. Dogs also featured in his request. Having a complete knowledge of the area, the inspector made arrangements for local isolated places to be searched at once and himself patrolled the lanes on both sides of the tracks. Local beat officers arriving to assist were despatched to patrol the surrounding district.

The first Criminal Investigation Department officer to arrive at the scene was the senior CID officer in Aylesbury Division at the time of the robbery, his detective inspector being on leave. He arrived at Cheddington at about 5.10 a.m. and commenced to make enquiries generally of the GPO and railway staff there. He saw the assistant chief constable and the detective superintendent at the scene some time later. He says about 5.40 a.m., but the exact time must have been around 6 a.m. They left again about 7.30 a.m.

Two officers of the Fingerprint and Photographic Department, Buckinghamshire Constabulary headquarters arrived at the scene at 6.30 a.m. and commenced to examine the attacked portion of the train. This comprised the diesel engine, high-valued packet coach and the parcels van which had been put on to the Aylesbury loop line at Cheddington. It was a tremendous task and whilst the examination was in progress they were called to Sears Crossing signal gantry where they spent some time examining the signals and batteries used by the thieves and taking photographs. They then returned to Cheddington and continued their examination of the attacked portion of the train. They were later informed that New Scotland Yard were going to be called in and that they were to take all the necessary photographs of the engine, train, station, Bridego Bridge, signals and other evidence left on the tracks. At this time their examination of the train was not complete.

Some time after 10 a.m. the detective superintendent showed the chief constable of Buckinghamshire over the scene. British Railways Police and GPO Investigation Branch officers also arrived at Cheddington.

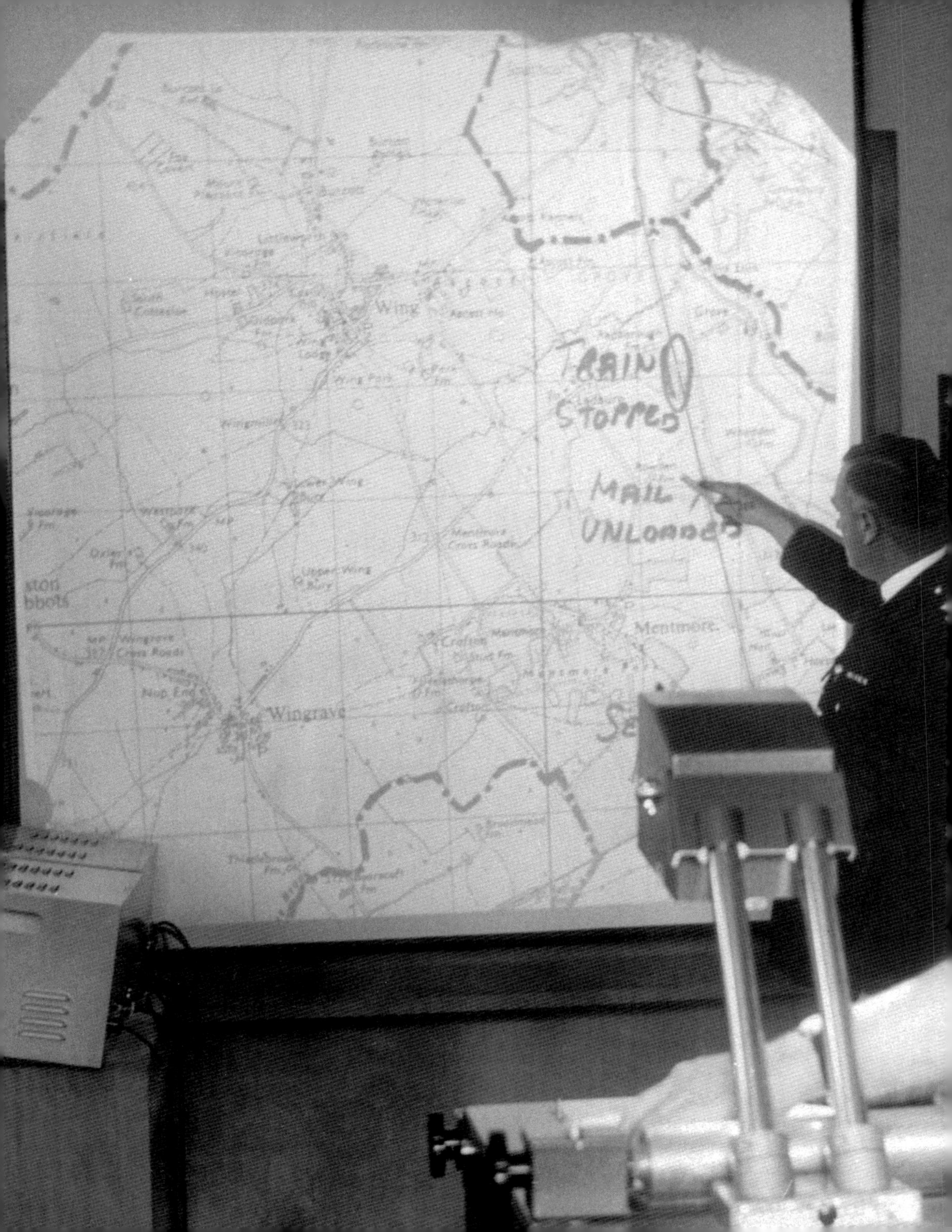
TRAIN
STOPPED
MAIL
UNLOADED
Wing
Wingrave
Mentmore

The investigation between 8th August and the discovery of Leatherslade Farm on 13th August 1963

HANDLING OF EXHIBITS

When the police were first called to the scene of the robbery it was soon realized that a large and serious crime had been committed, but the full magnitude of the act and the subsequent vast amount of enquiries were not fully appreciated. As far as exhibits were concerned they reached numbers which were never envisaged at the outset.

The start of the collection began at the actual scene of the robbery on the morning of the 8th August 1963. It was apparent from the start that there would be a number of articles to be collected and therefore the recording and labelling had to be accurate, precise and immediate. A detective constable was put in charge of this task and the method adopted is described later.

THE SETTING UP OF AN INCIDENT ROOM

It was fortunate that the Buckinghamshire Constabulary should have been equipped with a new police headquarters prior to the robbery for this provided, within 10 miles of the scene of the attack, a building equipped with modern amenities. The incident room was set up in the conference room which already had installed two telephones, one internal and the other a GPO line. The GPO without delay arranged for three additional outside lines to be connected to the Aylesbury headquarters switchboard and for one direct line into the incident room, to direct the enquiry, for two extensions from the incident room to the switchboard, one extension to the office of the officer in charge of the investigations

Large-scale map at local Scotland Yard headquarters showing the scene of the robbery, the point where the mailbags were unloaded and the search area which yielded the robbers' hideout and one extension to the exhibit room. (The incident room is fully described later.)

THE FIRST AND EARLY DAYS

At about 8.30 a.m. 8th August 1963, the controller of the GPO Investigation Branch telephoned the chief constable of Buckinghamshire and it was agreed that a meeting should be held of all interested parties at GPO Headquarters, London at 3 p.m. that day.

At 10.33 a.m. 8th August 1963 a message was sent to New Scotland Yard, and to the chief constables of Bedfordshire, Berkshire, Hertfordshire, Oxfordshire and Northamptonshire. The message was as follows:

> At approximately 0245 hours today a mail train robbery occurred between Leighton Buzzard and Cheddington, Bucks. 120 mailbags containing a very considerable sum of money are missing.
>
> It is thought that persons responsible may have hidden up and attempt to get away by mingling with normal morning traffic.
>
> Observation and frequent spot checks of traffic vehicles is requested.

During the morning of 8th August, the chief constable of Buckinghamshire telephoned the commander at New Scotland Yard, asking that New Scotland Yard be represented at a meeting of GPO and other organizations involved in the train robbery at 3 p.m. that afternoon at GPO Headquarters, London. This was agreed.

At 3 p.m. a conference was held at the Head Office of the GPO in London and among about 30 persons present were:

The chief constable of Buckinghamshire Constabulary and

representatives of his staff, including the detective
superintendent.
The head of the Criminal Investigation Department, New
Scotland Yard, and representatives of his staff.
The director of the Postal Services Department, General Post
Office, and representatives of his staff.
The controller, Investigation Branch, General Post Office and
representatives of his staff.
The chief of police (CID), British Transport Police and
representatives of his staff.

The chief constable of Buckinghamshire and the detective superintendent told the gathering of the information in their possession
regarding the robbery and the enquiries being conducted. It was
believed the theft would be in the region of two-and-a-half million
pounds.

At the conclusion of the meeting it was made clear that a detec-
tive superintendent and detective sergeant would be sent to
Aylesbury to assist in the enquiries, where they arrived at 10.20 p.m.
No minutes of this meeting were made.

Meanwhile at Buckinghamshire force headquarters, Aylesbury,
the staff were busy dealing with messages received from the public as the robbery had already been reported on in broadcasts by
the BBC. It will be remembered that in the early part of this
report, the fireman on the attacked train saw after the attack what
he described as a 10-ton army-type lorry (later amended to 5 tons).
This matter will be referred to again, particularly in view of the
following message received at Aylesbury force headquarters from
Linslade sub-division at 6 p.m. 8th August 1963.

Re: Mail Robbery. About 1.20 a.m. 8th August 1963, three vehicles were seen on the Cublington–Aston Abbotts Road, travelling

towards Aston Abbotts. All three vehicles were in close convoy. They are described as – a small vehicle, an army-type lorry, large wheels exposed, and a light land rover.

The persons giving the information were seen and statements taken.

On arrival at Aylesbury, the two CID officers at once made themselves conversant with the enquiries made and action taken. They arranged for road checks to be made the following morning for a period of two hours, commencing at one hour before the time of the robbery to one hour after the time of the robbery. It was hoped by this means to trace regular travellers in the area who might have seen something which could assist enquiries. They also conferred with several local farmers and with the aid of an Ordnance Survey map examined the area surrounding the scene of the robbery. Deserted farms and outbuildings, and ex-RAF and army camps likely to be used by the thieves as a hideout were pointed out to them.

This no doubt resulted in the following message being sent out by telex from Buckinghamshire headquarters at 9.30 a.m. 9th August 1963 to the chief constables of Bedfordshire, Hertfordshire, Northamptonshire and to divisions in Buckinghamshire – with an added note that similar searches be made throughout Buckinghamshire.

Ref: Railway Robbery
Bearing in mind possibility that the stolen mailbags might still be concealed within a reasonable distance of Cheddington, would you please continue the searches you have already organized of derelict farm buildings, barns, disused railway bridges, canal barges and other likely places. In addition to mailbags we are interested in a 10-ton army lorry and a light blue or grey

long wheel base land rover with hard top. One of these vehicles may have a broken wing mirror.

On Friday 9th August 1963, senior CID officers conferred over the steps already taken in the investigation and those which were needing to be put immediately into effect. The threat to the driver, the fireman and the GPO employees left in the high-valued packets coach that someone would be watching it for 30 minutes was noted. It was decided that was possibly the time which the thieves had allowed themselves to get clear away from the scene of the robbery to their hideout and if this was so the maximum distance they could have travelled would be in the region of 15 to 30 miles.

The possibility of being able, even with maximum help, to search such a vast area in an attempt to locate the thieves before they vacated their hideout and destroyed any evidence it may have contained was discussed. They believed it to be an impossible task but decided to announce their beliefs that the hideout was within 30 miles to press and radio reporters, knowing full well that great publicity would be given to it and hoping thereby to disturb the thieves, making them abandon their hideout before they were ready, possibly being caught doing so, or at the very least making them leave behind valuable clues which would assist the enquiry. The announcement to the press was made on the 9th August 1963. (This appeared as a second feature in the *London Evening Standard* on 10th August 1963.) There is no evidence that any roadblocks were set up to catch the thieves in view of this announcement.

One CID officer remained at Buckinghamshire Constabulary headquarters to assist in the setting up of the incident room for operational work and the installing of office equipment etc., whilst the two detective superintendents left headquarters to examine the scene.

On their arrival there it was discovered that the engine and the first coach behind it had been taken away from the sidings at Cheddington and their location was unknown. As an officer of the Fingerprint Branch was attending at Cheddington to further examine the engine, parcels van and high-valued packets coach, enquiries were at once put in hand to trace them. The parcels van was traced to Windermere and the engine to Crewe. These were returned to Cheddington on Saturday 10th August 1963.

From enquiries made about this it would appear that instructions had been given for the diesel engine, parcels coach and high-valued packets coach to remain at Cheddington for the time being. However, the British Transport Police were anxious to get the diesel engine and parcels van back into service. In the absence of any senior officer at Cheddington on the 8th August they were allowed to go.

Later on 9th August 1963, conferences were held at County Police headquarters Aylesbury with officers of the British Transport Police and members of the GPO Investigation Branch. All information was pooled and it was decided that certain enquiries could be conducted by them. The GPO investigating officers were to take statements from the GPO employees engaged on the train, other than those in the high-valued packets coach, from whom statements had already been taken, and the Railway Police were to seek out as much information as they could from their staff employed on the line.

In the meantime Buckinghamshire had circulated a message on behalf of British Railways as to future action to be taken by railway employees should a travelling post office train be unaccountably delayed in any section between signal boxes.

Following the message sent out to some of the surrounding counties from Buckinghamshire at 9.30 a.m. 9th August 1963 respecting the 10-ton army lorry seen by the fireman of the travelling post office, an express message was circulated at 5.35 p.m. on

9th August 1963 from New Scotland Yard. The information respecting the three vehicles seen in convoy, as passed to Buckinghamshire force headquarters from Linslade at 6 p.m. 8th August 1963 was not circulated until 8.46 p.m. 10th August 1963. This information was also passed to press and radio and Independent Television networks for transmission on the programme *Police Five*. At Leatherslade Farm were found three vehicles: an army 5-ton truck and two land rovers.

The pond alongside Bridego Bridge is fished by about 180 members of the Berkhamsted Angling Society. Each was seen in an effort to find out if, under the guise of an angler, a member of the gang had fished or pretended to do so whilst observing movements on the railway track. This produced no information of interest but it is a fact that Cordrey, one of the first two men arrested in connection with the crime, was found in possession of fishing tackle, and although he denies fishing in this particular pond he admitted fishing near Oxford, where it is known he spent two nights after the robbery.

At 12.30 a.m. on 11th August 1963, officers from C11 (Criminal Intelligence) Department, New Scotland Yard, visited the detective superintendent sent earlier to Aylesbury. They told him they had received information that Bobby Welch (identical with Robert Alfred Welch, CRO No. 61730/58, subsequently arrested and convicted for the robbery) was one of the gang responsible for the robbery. They said that Welch was missing from home and that his wife had received a message that he would be at home in two or three days' time. In addition, their information was that the thieves anticipated having 20 minutes in which to leave the scene of the robbery and get safely to their hideout before the alarm was raised.

The hideout was believed to be a farm owned by a man who dealt in horses and was somewhere on the outskirts of Aylesbury. Before C11 officers left Aylesbury arrangements were made with them for observation to be kept on Welch's home and two of his associates. (This work of C11 in connection with the train robbery is mentioned later.) Welch's finger impressions were subsequently identified by an officer of the Fingerprint Branch, New Scotland Yard, as being on articles at Leatherslade Farm.

The remainder of that night was spent studying maps and deciding which particular farms and small-holdings should be visited. This was not a particularly easy task as Buckinghamshire, particularly around Aylesbury, is agricultural and literally has hundreds of farms and small-holdings. The question of using servicemen from local camps to assist in searches was considered. As it was Bank Holiday week and also a weekend, camps had only skeleton staffs. It was decided to rely entirely on police manpower.

At 9 a.m. Sunday 11th August 1963 about 80 uniformed and Criminal Investigation Department personnel, drawn from Buckinghamshire and a contingent from Hertfordshire Constabulary, reported at Buckinghamshire force headquarters where they were briefed. A total of 13 likely premises had been selected as possible hideouts for the thieves (one of these in Hertfordshire) and these were all searched (by authority of warrants). By mid-day the searches had been completed. No success was reported. In most cases it was not necessary to use the warrants and following visits to the specified premises certain others which came to notice as a result of suggestions were also visited with the same result.

At 9.27 p.m. 11th August 1963, the following message was circulated to surrounding forces from New Scotland Yard and Buckinghamshire Constabulary:

Attention of all foot and mobile patrols is drawn to the fact that the money may be moved at night either in bulk or in part.

The next day, Monday 12th August 1963, a sergeant from

Aylesbury Division and 10 men searched a strip of land and buildings between grid lines 17 and 22. The search was in a westerly direction from Cheddington. The searchers gathered and set off about 11 a.m. They had instructions to search in strength, which was translated as five per building. They had a wireless vehicle which remained in sight of both parties, a wise precaution having regard to the likely number of thieves to be encountered.

On returning to his divisional headquarters at Aylesbury at 8 p.m. that night the sergeant reported he had reached the village of Quainton, the enormity of the task in hand, and that if the search was to be completed quickly more search teams were required. As a result, two further teams similarly composed and from a neighbouring division were formed. One team was to search the area to the north of and parallel to the one already being searched, and the other to the south. It will be noted here that all the searches arranged were to the west of Cheddington.

It was on the 13th August 1963 that Leatherslade Farm was discovered. Two of the teams organized to make searches on this day were disbanded; the remaining team was diverted to Leatherslade Farm.

At 12.50 p.m. on 12th August 1963, the following telephone message was recorded between the officer in charge of the investigation and the Bedfordshire force headquarters:

Told him what we are doing about searching likely places and what Herts. are doing. Would you do same?
Yes. Have already sent out some instruction – will do some more.

The action of surrounding forces will be dealt with under a separate heading.

On the afternoon of Monday 12th August 1963, a conference was held at Hertfordshire County headquarters. As a result of a suggestion made at this conference, the following message was circulated to all divisions in Buckinghamshire and to the chief constables of Hertfordshire County, Bedfordshire County and Northamptonshire County at 10.30 p.m.:

Reference to mail robbery

Bearing in mind that premises might have been specifically purchased or rented for use for the immediate concealment of the stolen property and its transport, please have enquiries made of estate agents and obtain information of transactions during the past six months involving likely premises within 30 miles of Cheddington, particularly farms, derelict houses, etc. Please follow up where appropriate.

Although certain other matters occurred relating to Leatherslade Farm on Monday 12th August 1963, these will be covered at a later stage when Leatherslade Farm is dealt with.

The action of surrounding forces

THE METROPOLITAN POLICE FLYING SQUAD

Following the report of the train robbery on the morning of 8th August 1963, a detective inspector was re-allocated from an Essex case, to which he had been put the previous day, to deal exclusively with enquiries directed to the squad and/or divisions of the Metropolitan Police concerning the train robbery. An incident room was set up for the squad manned by two officers who, under this detective inspector, were responsible for collating, logging and seeing that attention was given to all information received at New Scotland Yard. Some matters were given personal attention by the detective inspector and/or passed to the Flying Squad for attention. As the action by the Metropolitan Police will be covered in a separate section, only certain matters will be mentioned here. At least 18 Flying Squad officers and often as many as 30 were working exclusively on matters relating to the train robbery. Teams were putting in a minimum of 18 hours per day per man. There was daily liaison with COC1; the detective chief superintendent with overall responsibility for Flying Squad activities had directed that no matter what enquiries officers or teams had in hand, they were at all times to give priority to the train robbery case.

On Sunday 10th August 1963 the head of the incident room visited Aylesbury to liaise with the senior CID officers on progress and to inform them of efforts at the London end.

HERTFORDSHIRE

Hertfordshire, having received an initial message at 4.45 a.m. 8th August 1963, informed all mobiles and beat officers in the Hemel Hempstead Division which borders Buckinghamshire. Certain road checks were held, principally on main roads adjoining Bucking-hamshire. Records of the specific places were unfortunately destroyed after six months but the liaison officer appointed to deal with train robbery enquiries, a detective sergeant for Hertfordshire, was confident they were local in character and not maintained for any length of time. Nothing specific came of the checks.

On 9th August specific information concerning named persons and premises were received which were followed up and dealt with.

The Hertfordshire daily crime information for 10th August made reference to the robbery and made reference to the fact that the thieves could well be hiding out in the county.

On Sunday 11th August an inspector, two sergeants and eight constables went to Aylesbury for briefing in connection with the Sunday searches of farms. This party searched one farm only near Tring. The Hertfordshire police made use of RAF Police resources to search the RAF station at Bovingdon.

On the 12th August, following a request from the detective chief superintendent, Hertfordshire, a conference was held at Hatfield, which, amongst other things, resulted in searches being formalized and instituted to take in that part of Hertfordshire lying adjacent to the Buckinghamshire County boundary with particular reference to Cheddington. Search teams were formed and carried out searches of areas which were shaded on an Ordnance map, as they were completed, by the liaison officer. It was at this meeting also that the detective chief superintendent of Hertfordshire suggested that enquiries should be made of estate agents.

On 13th August a message was received in Hertfordshire asking that the searches be discontinued as Leatherslade Farm had been found. Hertfordshire however made further searches on the 14th August on an adjusted area, following on information put forward

by a GPO investigator which suggested that premises at Stanstead Abbotts, a small village in Hertfordshire, may also be involved.

BEDFORDSHIRE

In Bedfordshire, following first information from Buckinghamshire by wireless monitor at 4.38 a.m. 8th August 1963, road checks were held at Ampthill and on the A5. All patrolling vehicles and divisions of the force were informed. At 4.52 a.m. a further message from Buckinghamshire confirmed the serious nature of the offence. All divisions were then asked to put on road checks, although the precise location and duration of these is not clear.

On the 10th August 1963 a memorandum was sent out from Bedfordshire headquarters addressed to the superintendents of the 'B', 'C', 'D' and 'E' divisions of that force, asking that a thorough search be made of all derelict farm buildings, farms, disused railway bridges etc. in the county. Beat officers were also asked to seek the cooperation of farmers in finding farm premises recently let. The Dunstable Division, which borders the scene of the crime, made a thorough search of that division using two cars manned by eight men. They were employed exclusively on that task until it was completed.

A second memorandum to the Bedfordshire force on 12th August 1963 extended the area search to the Ampthill Division. This was further extended on 13th August to cover the Bedford Division. A third memorandum was sent out to the force extending enquiries to caravan sites and estate agents.

At 3.40 p.m. 13th August, Bedfordshire was asked to discontinue the search as the hideout of the thieves had been located at Brill in Buckinghamshire. Bedfordshire officers were not at any time asked to attend a conference. They would have been willing to have sent both uniformed and Criminal Investigation Department officers to Buckinghamshire had they been asked.

OXFORDSHIRE

This county boundary is only a short distance away from Leatherslade Farm. An Oxfordshire officer contacted Buckinghamshire on the morning of the robbery at 9.30 a.m. as no information had been received from Buckinghamshire about the robbery. The head of the Criminal Investigation Department offered the loan of uniformed and Criminal Investigation Department personnel. This offer was later confirmed by the chief constable of Oxfordshire (since deceased) when he spoke to Buckinghamshire headquarters himself. The offer was not taken up by Buckinghamshire.

Oxfordshire received the message sent out from Buckinghamshire at 10.33 a.m. 8th August asking for frequent spot checks. This brought queries from their divisions as to specifically where and when in relation to the crime. No 30-mile radius was discussed with this force. Searches were however made of derelict and unused buildings and these were reported accordingly.

The chief constable of Oxfordshire took a great personal interest in all that his force did regarding the robbery, saw a copy of everything sent to Buckinghamshire and had a summary prepared of all enquiries made.

Leatherslade Farm

Leatherslade Farm is on the Brill beat and in the Waddesdon section of the Buckinghamshire Constabulary. It is within two miles of the Oxfordshire border and in the parish of Oakley.

The last owner bought Leatherslade Farm in July 1952 and lived there until 7th July 1963. The house was put up for sale in either February or March 1963, when it was placed in the hands of three estate agents in Oxfordshire.

Towards the end of May 1963, the owner received a telephone call from a London solicitor saying he had a client who wished to buy the property and who would pay the money immediately in cash. The owner was led to believe that of two men who had called at the farm a day or two previously, one was the prospective purchaser and the other his managing clerk.

The owner consulted his solicitors and eventually a price of £5,550 was agreed on. He understood that a deposit of £555 (10%) had been paid to the agents and agreed with his solicitors that the purchaser could have possession of the premises when full settlement was made. He was later given to understand that full settlement could not be made until 13th August 1963, because the purchaser's money would not be available until that date. The purchaser still wished to take possession of the premises by 29th July 1963, and finally it was agreed he could take over on that date, providing he paid 7% interest on the balance owing to cover the mortgage on the new property the owner was buying.

The owner left the farm on Sunday 7th July 1963 but left his parents and the majority of the furniture in the house. They moved out on 29th July 1963. Before leaving the house he had a telephone call from a 'Mr Field' asking him to leave the key. By

The farmhouse of the abandoned Leatherslade Farm

arrangement this was left with a resident of Oakley, Buckinghamshire.

To describe the premises as a farm is something of a misnomer. It consists in fact of a cottage which has been rebuilt and renovated so that two families may separately occupy it. This was the position prior to the robbery, when the owner and his family lived in the main part of the cottage whilst his parents occupied the remainder. Five acres of land made up the small-holding which stands on a rise almost directly below Brill, but which itself looks down on the Oxford–Thame Road, B4011, and commands an excellent view of the surrounding countryside and approach roads.

The premises are not easily seen from the main road and in fact when full foliage covers surrounding trees and hedges, as was the case at the time of the robbery, they cannot be seen. There is only one entrance direct from the Thame Road, whence a rough but hard surface track about 300 yards in length and rising brings the visitor to the premises proper. To the north of the living accommodation there are outbuildings which need only the description that they were exactly sufficient to contain and conceal the five-ton lorry and two land rover vehicles which were used and left there by the thieves.

The previous owner had not, it would seem, been a particularly tidy occupier and his interest in motorcycling left a good many items of motorcycle bric-a-brac littering the outbuildings. The ground and gardens generally were not particularly well kept and indeed his main business interest appears to have been in buying and selling greengrocery and similar produce from markets.

At the entrance and near the main road a barn and other buildings house a milking unit. These are owned by a local farmer and are generally run on his behalf by a herdsman, who played a part in directing attention to Leatherslade Farm. It is worth mentioning here that Leatherslade Farm is marked on the Ordnance

Survey map under another name. Locally it is more generally referred to as 'X's place'. It was known as such to the local police officer at Brill whose duties and action at the time of the robbery are referred to later. He knew of the premises as he had visited them previously on a local enquiry.

In the district it appears to have been fairly common knowledge that there were plans to dispose of the premises, but this had been mooted for some months and there was nothing specific known as to the date of disposal or who was likely to buy.

Events leading up to and the discovery of Leatherslade Farm

The first occasion on which the farm was specifically brought to the notice of the police as being a likely hideout for the thieves was late on Sunday 11th August 1963, when the head of the Oxfordshire County CID had a conversation with an informant in an Oxfordshire club. It was mentioned during the conversation that 'X's place' at Oakley was a likely spot as a hideout for the thieves as it was isolated and in a little-known situation. It was known to the informant, as he had met the previous owner in connection with their joint interest in motorcycle meetings and socially. He knew the farm was up for sale and so far as he was aware had not been sold up to a few days before the robbery. The informant described it as merely a hunch on his part.

The following day the head of Oxfordshire County CID made some enquiries to verify the information he had been given. On being satisfied that the information given to him was true and that the previous owner was in fact living in Dunsdon, Berkshire, he telephoned the following message to Aylesbury at 11.47 p.m. 12th August 1963.

> Whilst making enquiries at Wheatley, Oxfordshire, re mail robbery, information was received that the premises at Leatherslade Farm, Brill, Bucks were in the market for some time with no prospective purchaser. These premises were purchased a few weeks ago for a large sum of money. The informant suggested that this may be of interest to the robbery.

This message was received by a police constable in the operations

Equipment found by police in Leatherslade farmhouse – including sleeping bags, kitchen kits and tinned food

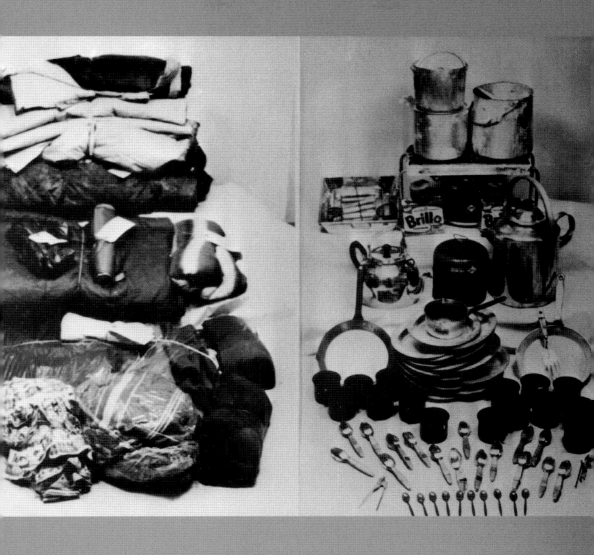

room, Aylesbury force headquarters.

At 9 a.m. 12th August 1963, the police constable on duty in the incident room at police headquarters, Aylesbury, received a telephone call from a herdsman concerning his suspicions that Leatherslade Farm may have been the 'hideout' of the train robbery gang. He made a message of this information and handed it to the senior CID officer. There is no trace of this message anywhere and it was not acted on.

The herdsman was away on holiday from 26th July until 4th August 1963. From the 4th August onwards he saw nothing happening at Leatherslade Farm to arouse his suspicions. On Monday 12th August, after reading his morning paper, which mentioned that police were interested in isolated farms in connection with the train robbery, and knowing that Leatherslade Farm had been vacated, he went to the farm. He noticed the curtains were drawn and that a large lorry was parked in one of the outbuildings. These facts made him suspicious and he telephoned the police.

At 9.05 a.m. 13th August 1963, the police sergeant of Waddesdon, on whose section Leatherslade Farm was situated, received a message from Buckinghamshire headquarters incident room, informing him that a telephone message had been received the night before that Leatherslade Farm, Brill, had been sold recently for a high price and would he examine the place. (This information was passed to Waddesdon as a result of the telephone message from the head of Oxfordshire County CID.) The sergeant had never heard of Leatherslade Farm and contacted the police constable at Brill, and another police constable who had previously worked the Brill beat. Neither knew Leatherslade Farm. The Brill constable was of the opinion it referred to a farm at Oakley known to him as X's place. Whilst these discussions were taking place the Waddesdon sergeant received a further call from Buckinghamshire headquarters incident room that the herdsman had telephoned again respecting Leatherslade Farm. (This message was not recorded in the incident room at Buckinghamshire headquarters, the reason being that the same police constable was on duty in the incident room who had received the first call. He assured the herdsman that attention was being given to it.) It was as a result of this call that more information was given as to the whereabouts of the farm. The Waddesdon sergeant met the Brill constable at 10.30 a.m. 13th August and went to Leatherslade Farm, where they arrived at 10.50 a.m. They conferred with the herdsman and then examined the farm. They found that it had indeed been the hideout of the thieves and that mailbags were hidden in the basement. The sergeant telephoned Buckinghamshire force headquarters at 11.45 a.m. and returned to the farm.

ACTION AT THE FARM

At the time the Waddesdon sergeant telephoned the Buckinghamshire force headquarters, giving the information that Leatherslade Farm had no doubt been used as a hideout for the thieves, the head of CID and the detective chief superintendent in charge of the Flying Squad activities were at Buckinghamshire force headquarters. They had spent two hours that morning discussing the crime and investigations made to date with the senior CID officers in charge and later with the chief constable. In view of the weight of work connected with the administration and organization of the enquiry it was decided after these consultations that the services of more metropolitan officers were needed, and four officers of the Metropolitan Police arrived at Aylesbury that afternoon.

Immediately the information about Leatherslade Farm was received at Buckinghamshire force headquarters, the chief constable of Buckinghamshire, the assistant chief constable of Buckinghamshire, the head of CID, the detective chief superintendent in charge of Flying Squad activities and other senior CID officers left for Leatherslade Farm, where they arrived at about 1.30 p.m.

Arrangements were made at once for the farm to be adequately guarded to ensure that no unauthorized person visited there until an examination by experts from the Forensic Laboratory and Fingerprint Department, New Scotland Yard, had been made. Accordingly one of the search teams was directed to Leatherslade Farm for guard duties. The farm was under guard until Sunday 25th August 1963. In addition the GPO connected the farm with two outside telephones. An incident room was set up at Brill Police Station and remained in being from the 13th to 16th August 1963.

From 2.10 p.m. 14th August, in addition to enquiries being made in the locality of Leatherslade Farm, the public address system was used on a police wireless vehicle, and 17 villages were covered. The text of the message broadcast was as follows:

> Can you help the police? Can you give us any information about the recent occupants of Leatherslade Farm or about activities at the farm in the past two weeks? If so please call at Brill Police Station or telephone Brill 802.

In addition, when Leatherslade Farm was found the news appeared on television and radio. As can be imagined this resulted in a lot of information being telephoned to Brill.

One most important piece of information was given by a resident of Brill Road, Oakley, on 14th August 1963, to the effect that she retired to bed at about 10 p.m. 7th August 1963. She awoke about midnight and as she could not sleep she got up and walked to the window which faces Thame Road and Leatherslade Farm – Leatherslade Farm is about half a mile away. After only a few minutes her attention was drawn to a bright light on a vehicle in Thame Road. As it approached the Brill Road, the light was dimmed. She then noticed that a solo motor cycle, a covered van and another motor vehicle had turned right into Brill Road. They passed in front of her house in the direction of Brill. She woke again about 4 a.m. and could not get back to sleep and at about 4.30 a.m. she heard the sound of approaching vehicles. She again went to the window and saw a solo motor cycle, a covered van and another vehicle coming from the direction of Brill. She was certain they were the same vehicles she had seen earlier. They passed the front of her house and turned left into Thame Road in the direction of Leatherslade Farm. They were showing only very dim lights and she then lost sight of them.

A number of other local people were able to speak of vehicles being seen at various times in the vicinity of Leatherslade Farm. The licensee of a public house which is about three miles from Brill spoke of five men, all strangers and travelling in a 'posh car', visiting his public house on Saturday 10th August 1963. They stated they were very hungry and enquired the way to Brill. They refused to accept their change.

The remainder of the 13th August was taken up by the investigating officers in arranging for the attendance of experts at the farm, interviewing and taking statements at Brill and generally supervising work at both incident rooms.

On the 14th August a detective superintendent (since retired), two inspectors and a senior photographer from the Fingerprint Branch, New Scotland Yard, commenced an examination of Leatherslade Farm where they remained for three days. They collected 243 photographs of scene of crime marks made up of 311 fingers and 56 bits of palm. They also removed from the farm for further examination at New Scotland Yard 1,534 bank envelopes, a number of newspapers and other loose items.

Two chief inspectors and four laboratory staff from the Forensic Science Laboratory, New Scotland Yard, also attended on

14th August and remained for three days. They were joined on the third day by an expert from the laboratory. The farm was again visited on 28th September in connection with paint found on one of the shoes of a prisoner who was arrested at a later stage. The work and success of these two departments will be covered later.

The department at New Scotland Yard dealing with thefts of motor vehicles, C10, was also called in and an examination was made at Leatherslade Farm of the three vehicles found there and abandoned by the train robbers. Within a very short time the complete history of each vehicle had been adduced. Two had been purchased and one stolen by the thieves.

After the initial enquiries into the purchase of Leatherslade Farm had been made, all documents were handed over to a member of the Company Fraud Squad (C6), New Scotland Yard, with a special knowledge of conveyancing, and he was instructed by the head of CID to continue enquiries. This matter is referred to later when the two Fields and Wheater were arrested.

When the Brill constable first visited the farm on the 13th August 1963, he saw in an open-fronted shed an army-type 3-ton motor lorry. It was partly covered with a green tarpaulin sheet. He could see that, although most of the vehicle was coloured khaki-green, the cab had recently been hand-painted yellow. In a padlocked garage at the far end of the house he saw a land rover parked. He saw another land rover in another padlocked garage situated some yards back down the driveway. In the yard he also saw the remains of a bonfire. There were charred pieces of clothing, food tins and what appeared to be metal fittings from army equipment. In the front garden was a partly dug pit. After gaining access to the house, by way of a partly open bedroom window, he saw on the floor in a downstairs room some bedding, comprising two sleeping bags and a blanket. In the kitchen were various items of camping equipment and cutlery. In an alcove

A mailbag container being wheeled into a travelling post office

between the kitchen and the sitting room he saw two fruit crates and a sack of potatoes. They were standing on a wooden trapdoor. The trapdoor was lifted and gave access to steps leading into a cellar; on examining the cellar he found a number of full sacks, one of which he identified as a GPO mailbag. It was not fastened and contained banknote wrappers and bank papers. Another sack contained articles of clothing.

Between the 14th and 19th August a number of photographs were taken at the farm and at Buckinghamshire Constabulary headquarters by a police photographer of the Buckinghamshire Constabulary. These best describe the situation at Leatherslade Farm. An exhibits officer also visited the farm on a number of occasions and took possession of all exhibits, which were then listed.

The general investigation and procedure leading to the arrest of the thieves and receivers

It is not intended under this heading to give all the mass of detail which led to the successful investigation of the crime as much of it was routine, but to concentrate on certain aspects and matters which appear to be of interest and about which some comment will be made in the summary of recommendations and interesting features. Other matters for comment have been covered under particular headings showing the other facets of the investigation.

Following on the visit of the head of CID and the detective chief superintendent responsible for Flying Squad activities to Aylesbury and Leatherslade Farm on the 13th August 1963, it was decided that the detective chief superintendent of No. 1 District Metropolitan Police should take over all outside enquiries in connection with the train robbery. In particular he should concentrate on seeking for and arresting the robbers, whilst the CID officer and his staff at Aylesbury should concentrate on the preparation of evidence against them and compilation of the reports for the director of public prosecutions. This was a formidable task in view of the enormity of the offence, the great number of witnesses and the vast amount of exhibits found at Leatherslade Farm and on the railway tracks. Accordingly as from 9 a.m. 14th August 1963, the aforementioned detective chief superintendent of the Metropolitan Police was placed in charge of the whole operation.

The total amount of monies stolen on the train robbery was £2,595,997 10s. contained in 636 packages which in turn were in 120 mailbags. Eight mailbags containing high-valued packets were left behind in the high-valued packets coach by the thieves. The total amount of monies recovered to date is £336,518.

The first matter of importance after the discovery of Leatherslade Farm was the arrest of Roger John Cordrey, CRO 3716/42, 42 years, florist, no fixed abode, and William Gerald Boal, CRO 30624/47, 49 years, engineer, Fulham, London SW6, at Bournemouth.

They were arrested at about 9 p.m. 14th August 1963 by officers of the Bournemouth police, following on information given to the police. On arrival at police headquarters at Bournemouth they were seen by the station sergeant in the charge room, searched in his presence, and the property found in their possession logged individually on the charge sheets. The property found in possession of each individual prisoner was placed in separate bags. Both prisoners refused to sign to the effect that the property had been taken from their possession.

Keys found in the possession of Boal were used to unlock an A35 car, UEL 987, in a garage in Tweedale Road, and a suitcase in the car which contained a quantity of banknotes. The amount of money found in the car was £56,047.

Another car, TLX 279, was found in a garage in Ensbury Avenue, Bournemouth. The garage was opened with a key found in Boal's possession. Six suitcases were found in the boot of the car. These contained £78,982.

At 3 a.m. 15th August 1963, a flat was searched in Wimborne Road, Bournemouth. In a bedroom there was found a briefcase containing banknotes and under a pillow on the bed was £840. The total money recovered from the flat was £5,910. The monies found in the cars and the flat were counted by two bank clerks from the National Provincial Bank Limited in Bournemouth. Both Boal and Cordrey admitted that the monies found had come from the train robbery, and the London addresses of the prisoners were subsequently searched by the Metropolitan Police (Flying Squad officer).

One of the men accused of the robbery being escorted under cover into court at Linslade

At the trial it was alleged that the property found on Boal and Cordrey had been mixed when they were searched. On Saturday 30th May 1964, enquiries were made at Bournemouth and the chief constable and later two other officers were seen, together with the charge sheets prepared when Boal and Cordrey were arrested. The whole of the procedure was gone through which showed that the prisoners were searched individually and their respective properties kept separate.

The ownership of the keys was contested by Boal as neither prisoner would sign for the property found in his possession. One of the officers was quite definite as to which property was found on each prisoner.

Following the arrests of Boal and Cordrey, the New Scotland Yard officer at Aylesbury was notified. He, together with a Buckinghamshire officer and another New Scotland Yard officer, arrived at Bournemouth at 4 a.m. 15th August 1963. Cordrey and Boal each made statements under caution, giving their version as to how the money came to be in their possession and their activities since the day of the train robbery.

Every precaution was taken to ensure the safe custody of the prisoners and property en route from Bournemouth to Aylesbury, where they arrived at 9.30 p.m. 15th August 1963. The money recovered was lodged in the safe in the chief constable's office at Aylesbury force headquarters and instruction given to officers on night duty in the incident room to visit the chief constable's office occasionally during each night.

At about 9 a.m. 16th August 1963, as a result of information received, a detective inspector of the Surrey Constabulary went to Coldharbour Lane, Leith, Surrey, where he took possession of a camel leather briefcase, a brown leather briefcase, a holdall and a brown leather suitcase. These cases contained £100,900.

A detective constable of the Surrey Constabulary examined the cases for fingerprints and whilst doing so he found in the camel leather briefcase an account from a Continental hotel. This account was in a narrow pocket in the silk lining, which was torn above the pocket. On the brown leather briefcase he found a number of finger impressions. These finger impressions and the case in its entirety were photographed by the Surrey Constabulary. All photographs taken were subsequently examined by the Fingerprint Branch at New Scotland Yard. The prints found were identified as those of Brian Field, and the hotel bill in his name was later tied down to him as a result of enquiries made in Germany, when it was proved that both he and his wife had stayed at a hotel there during the period to which the bill related. Field was arrested and convicted of conspiracy in the robbery (conviction quashed on appeal) and also a lesser conspiracy of attempting to obstruct the course of justice.

On Tuesday 13th August 1963 a sales assistant in a lady's dress shop in Reigate became suspicious of a woman customer who bought a quantity of clothing and paid in dirty £1 notes. The conduct of the woman was sufficiently suspicious to cause the shop assistant to follow her and note the number of a small grey sports car the woman got into as REN 22. On returning to the shop she immediately contacted the police. Two constables located the car and kept observations on it and subsequently saw a man who gave his name and address as James Edward Patten of The Woodlands, Beulah Hill, Croydon, SE19. He was accompanied by the woman who had been into the dress shop. After some conversation he satisfied the police constables and drove away.

Further enquiries were made by Reigate police and it was learned the couple had been to a number of shops and purchased goods. At one shop Patten had given his name as Mr Ballard, Clovelly Caravan Site, Bexhill Road, Boxhill, Surrey. This site was visited and it was learned that a man giving the name of Ballard

had on 11th August 1963 bought a caravan there. The caravan was searched and £136 in £1 notes was found in a jacket pocket.

Observations were kept on the caravan by Dorking officers and on 18th August 1963 a man was stopped entering the caravan. He was interviewed but there was insufficient evidence to arrest him. Subsequent enquiries identified Ballard and Patten as being James Edward White, CRO 26113/55, and a search of the panelling of the caravan revealed a large amount in notes which was counted by the manager and a clerk of the Midland Bank, Dorking. The amount was £30,440.

Some of the notes were identified as being part of the money stolen by the robbery. It was all handed over to investigating officers on 20th August 1963.

On 19th August 1963 a detective sergeant of C3 Department went to the caravan and examined it for fingerprints. He took possession of a number of articles on which he developed finger marks which have since been identified as those of White. A milk bottle was also taken possession of. The fingerprints upon it were photographed and submitted to C3 Department. They have been identified as being those of White.

On 21st August 1963 the caravan was taken to Aylesbury and remains under lock and key at Aylesbury headquarters. The money on arrival back at Aylesbury was placed in the chief constable's safe. It was handed to the bank manager who counted and identified all monies.

A thorough enquiry was made respecting the address given to the two police constables at Reigate. It was learned that the Pattens took tenancy of the house in Beulah Hill, SE19, on the 25th March 1962, at £295 per annum and paid their rent quarterly in advance. No payment had been made since the last quarterly payment commencing on 24th June 1963. Mrs Patten was last seen at the flat on 27th July 1963. On Monday 29th July 1963 Mr Patten

Banknotes stashed in the walls of the caravan owned by James White at Clovelly Caravan Site telephoned the daily woman and said that his wife had gone away on holiday. Nothing has been heard of them since at Beulah Hill.

The Austin Healey car REN 22 was purchased by a man giving the name of Mr John Steward, of Rock House, Chaunston Road, Taunton, Somerset (false), at 5.30 p.m. 9th August 1963, from a firm in King's Road, SW3, for £900. This was paid in cash in £5 notes. Steward has been identified as White. On 10th August 1963, an application was received by the London County Council for a 12-monthly licence commencing 10th August 1963 from James Edward Patten (since identified as White) of The Woodlands, Beulah Hill, SE19. The change of ownership of this vehicle to J.E. Patten was recorded by London County Council on this date.

On Wednesday 14th August 1963 a man since identified as White left the Austin Healey REN 22 at a garage in Aldersgate, EC1, for repair. He failed to collect it and on 21st August 1963 police removed the car to Chalk Farm police garage. James Edward White is still wanted for the robbery.

The three vehicles found abandoned at Leatherslade Farm were as follows. The first was a new land rover bearing false index plates BMG 757A. It was light blue in colour but overpainted khaki. The vehicle was later identified as having been stolen from Oxenden Street, London WC1, between 7.30 p.m. and 11 p.m. 21st July 1963. The vehicle when stolen was fitted with a radio set. The radio set was still in position, attached to the dashboard of the vehicle, when it was recovered.

The second was an ex-War Department land rover bearing index plates BMG 757A. This vehicle passed through the auction of ex-War Department vehicles at Ruddington, Notting-hamshire, on 2nd July 1963, and was sold to a London motor dealer. The vehicle had been resprayed a deep bronze green by the purchaser. This dealer re-sells their vehicles to the public through the medium of advertisements in the *Exchange and Mart*.

On 26th July the dealer received a telephone call about the vehicle and as a result two men called. One of them, who gave the name of Bentley, agreed to purchase the land rover for £195. The vehicle was registered and allocated the number BMG 757A. On 1st August 1963 Bentley telephoned the dealer, was given the number, and called to collect the vehicle with the registration number plate on either 3rd or 4th August 1963. He signed the duplicate receipt for the vehicle 'F. Wood p.p. C. Bentley'. Bentley was later identified as James E. White.

The third vehicle was an Austin goods platform truck bearing false index plates BPA 260. This vehicle when found was dark green in colour, with the front and cabin crudely overpainted yellow. It was traced as having passed through the auction of ex-War Department vehicles on 24th April 1963, and was purchased by a government surplus contractor in Edgware. They re-sprayed inside and out olive green. This vehicle was purchased by a man giving the name of F. Blake, 272 Kenton Lane, Middlesex (false), for £300. On 30th July 1963 Blake collected the vehicle, saying he had registered it. He had no index plate with him and chalked a registration number on the original blanks. This number could not be remembered. A man similar to Blake and referred to as 'Jimmy' by a second man was directed to the contractors by another firm in Edgware. 'Jimmy' later returned and said that he had bought a lorry. 'Jimmy' has been identified as James E. White.

The false number BPA 260 referred to a Ford car. This vehicle was broken up by a scrap dealer in Gloucester two or three years ago. The road fund licence displayed on the lorry relates to a vehicle VJD 35. The licence was stolen from this vehicle at Warner Place, London E2, between 7.30 p.m. 29th July 1963 and 2 p.m. 30th July 1963 and was reported to police at Bethnal Green on 30th July 1963.

This covers the activities relating to the arrest of Boal and

Cordrey on 14th August 1963; the finding of a number of cases containing money in Surrey, which produced evidence against Brian Arthur Field – whose later arrest later will be dealt with in sequence; the checking of James Edward White at Reigate by the two police constables of the Surrey Constabulary on the 13th August 1963, and the subsequent tracing of a caravan at Boxhill, Surrey, which had been bought by White and in which was found £30,576. The vehicles at Leatherslade Farm have been mentioned as White was identified as being instrumental in purchasing two of them.

Following the arrest of Boal and Cordrey four persons were arrested between 14th August and 21st August and charged with receiving certain monies connected with the train robbery.

On 22nd August 1963 Charles Frederick Wilson, CRO 5010/54, aged 31 years, a greengrocer of Clapham, London SW4, was arrested by Metropolitan Police Flying Squad officers and charged with being concerned in the robbery. This man had denied having been either to Cheddington or Leatherslade Farm. Wilson's finger and palm impressions were found at Leatherslade Farm, on the window-sill of the kitchen, on a 'Saxa' salt drum and on a cellophane wrapping of a 'Johnson's' traveller's kit, found in the kitchen.

A detective inspector and a detective sergeant of the Surrey Constabulary, stationed at Reigate, saw Ronald Biggs at his home in Redhill, Surrey, at 6.45 p.m. 24th August 1963, as it had come to notice that his wife was spending a lot of money. Biggs admitted winning £510 at the races, a fact which was verified. It was during this interview and after being asked if he knew any of the men who were wanted in connection with the train robbery in Buckinghamshire that he said 'I knew Reynolds some years ago. I met him when we were doing time together in Wandsworth.' Nothing of significance was found at the house.

One of the ransacked mail carriages on the travelling post office

On Wednesday 4th September 1963 at about 2.45 p.m. Ronald Arthur Biggs, CRO 40117/47, born 8th August 1929, a builder of Redhill, Surrey, was arrested at his home by Metropolitan Police Flying Squad officers and taken to New Scotland Yard where he was seen by the head of the Flying Squad. Biggs was asked a number of questions which were taken from a prepared questionnaire and the replies were written down. Biggs refused to sign the document. It was after Biggs was told he was being taken back to Aylesbury to be charged with being concerned with others in committing robbery that he was cautioned.

Fingerprints found on a Monopoly box, a blue-edged Pyrex plate and a bottle of ketchup found at the farmhouse were identified as those of Biggs. Biggs claimed he was at home on 7th/8th August 1963; he remembered the 8th August 1963 particularly because it was his birthday. He denied knowing the Cheddington district, Oakley or Brill or visiting Leatherslade Farm. Evidence of rebuttal was obtained should Biggs call evidence to say he was at home on the night of 7th/8th August 1963.

On the 7th September 1963 Metropolitan Police Flying Squad officers went to Dog Kennel Hill, London SE22, where they saw James Hussey, CRO 40455/49, born 8th April 1933, a painter. They had a search warrant to search his house in connection with the mail robbery. The search was conducted but nothing was found to connect Hussey with the offence. He was then taken to New Scotland Yard where he was seen by the head of the Flying Squad. He denied having had anything to do with the robbery and knowing or having visited Leatherslade Farm, Brill or Oakley. He also denied knowing any of the persons who had been charged with the robbery, or who had been circulated by the press as being wanted for it. A statement was taken from him under caution to this effect. He was then questioned about the land rover and the lorry which were used in commission of the robbery, but denied any knowledge of them. A statement was taken from him under caution confirming this.

Hussey was taken to Aylesbury where he was charged with being concerned with others in committing robbery. His palm and finger impressions were taken and later compared with marks found at Leatherslade Farm. The palm print of one of Hussey's hands was found to be identical with a palm print found on the tailboard of the Austin lorry – false plate BTA 260.

When the home of the prisoner Welch, who was arrested on 25th October 1963, was searched, a hotel bill in the name of Richards showing that five men stayed at a hotel in Nottingham, on the night of 22nd May 1963, was found in the sideboard. When this bill was examined for fingerprints by the Fingerprint Branch, New Scotland Yard, a print was found which was identified as that of James Hussey. Subsequently the hotel receptionist picked out Hussey at an identification parade at Aylesbury as being one of the five men who stayed at a hotel in Nottingham on 22nd May 1963. She could not say whether he was the man who gave the name of Richards. She was unable to make any other identification.

On the 11th September 1963 Thomas William Wisbey, CRO 26362/47, born 27th April 1930, of Camberwell, was taken to New Scotland Yard by Flying Squad officers. Wisbey was first seen by Flying Squad officers on the 20th August 1963, when he voluntarily visited New Scotland Yard. Wisbey explained his movements on 7th and 8th August 1963, which were taken down in the form of a statement which he signed; then Wisbey left New Scotland Yard.

On the 11th September 1963 Wisbey telephoned New Scotland Yard, and as a result he was seen by two Flying Squad officers and taken to New Scotland Yard where he was seen by the head of the Flying Squad. He denied knowing Brill, Oakley, Leatherslade Farm, any of the persons charged with the robbery, and any other person whose names and addresses had been in the papers and connected with the robbery. He made a statement under caution confirming his original one.

Wisbey was then told he was going to be charged with the robbery and cautioned. He was taken to Aylesbury and charged. His finger and palm prints were taken and forwarded to the Fingerprint Branch, New Scotland Yard, where they were compared with prints found at Leatherslade Farm. They were found to be identical with those found on an attachment to the bath at Leatherslade Farm.

On the 14th September 1963 Leonard Denis Field, CRO 20473/51, aged 31 years, a merchant seaman of Harringay, N4, was arrested by Metropolitan Police officers for the robbery. He was the man who was identified as the purchaser of Leatherslade Farm. Wheater – who will be mentioned later – designated Field as the purchaser of the farm on the contract. A deposit of £555 was paid on the purchase price of £5,550 on 23rd July 1963 and possession upon exchange of contracts and before completion was asked for and arranged for 29th July 1963. Wheater signed his half of the contract on behalf of his client which was most unusual. The self-evident effect of it is that any subsequent investigator is denied a sight of Leonard Field's signature.

The Fingerprint Branch, New Scotland Yard, examined a bank authority which Brian Field – managing clerk for Wheater, and no relation to Leonard Denis Field – had identified as bearing the signature of Leonard Field who negotiated for the farm. A fingerprint was found on the document which was identified as belonging to Leonard Denis Field. This fingerprint, together with the signature, established the identity of the prospective purchaser and owner of the document as Leonard Denis Field.

On the 15th September 1963 Brian Arthur Field, aged 28 years, a managing clerk (unqualified) of Whitchurch Hill, Oxfordshire, was arrested for the robbery by Metropolitan Police officers. It will be remembered that on 16th August 1963 a number of bags containing £100,900 in banknotes and connected with the robbery were found in Surrey. These were examined for fingerprints and on a briefcase a number of fingerprints were found which were later identified as those of Brian Arthur Field. In addition a hotel bill made out to Herr and Frau Field, relating to accommodation at Sonnenbiche Hotel, Hindelang, southern Germany between 2nd and 16th February 1963 was found in the lining of one of the cases. This was traced back as relating to Brian Arthur Field and his wife.

During the enquiries into the sale of Leatherslade Farm, the association of Leonard Denis Field, CRO 20473/51, and Brian Arthur Field was established. In addition the neighbours of Brian Arthur Field were able to say that on Friday evening 9th August 1963 a fair number of motor cars kept calling at Field's house. During the night they were unable to sleep owing to the number of cars calling at Field's residence. The traffic continued throughout Saturday into the small hours of Sunday morning. Field later spoke to his neighbours about the number of visitors he had had during the preceding days. He said something to the effect that the 'Brighton horse racing gangs case starts in September and that he represented them.'

To summarize the position, anyone who acquired Leatherslade Farm and remained in possession and control during the relevant period, in default of a watertight explanation, must be an accessory to the robbery. Anyone else assisting with guilty knowledge must be a party to conspiracy to rob. Brian Field, on his own admission, shortly before the robbery, examined the farm with a Leonard Field whom he knew to be the relation of a convicted criminal. Upon reading about the connection of the farm with the robbery, he made no effort to contact the police with his knowledge.

On the 17th October 1963 John Denby Wheater, born 17th

December 1921, a solicitor of Ashtead, Surrey, was arrested on warrant by Fraud and Flying Squad officers. The warrant contained two charges, briefly as follows:

(a) Conspiracy to stop a mail train with intent to rob, and
(b) Well knowing that one Leonard Denis Field, had stolen 120 mailbags, did comfort, harbour, assist and maintain him.

Wheater designated the purchaser of the farm on the *contract* as Leonard Field, of Earls Court Road, London SW5, and subsequently stated to the police that this was the address supplied by his client. The premises at Earls Court Road were part of the estate of a notorious property dealer, which is now administered on behalf of his widow by a company with registered offices in Southampton Row, London WC.

In March 1963 this company began negotiations to sell the house in Earls Court Road. Originally the purchasers were a partnership of three, but the partner put forward as the nominee purchaser withdrew, leaving the remaining two partners to carry on with the transaction. They decided to form a company for the purpose, and on 14th August 1963 an amended contract was signed on behalf of this company.

Wheater, who acted for one of the partners in a previous property deal, was instructed to act for the partnership in the purchase. He was also asked to look after the formation of their company, which was to be purchased, already incorporated, from a firm who deal in company registrations. A great deal more enquiry was made into these transactions and suffice it to say that the facts proved from the outset that Earls Court Road was a false address for Leonard Field; moreover that it was an address supplied by Wheater himself. Although the arrest of Wheater did not take place until the 17th October, I have included his arrest at this stage as he was closely

Police officers gathering evidence

connected with the facts surrounding the arrest of Leonard Denis Field and Brian Field.

On 1st October 1963 Martin Harvey, CRO 9249/57, born 23rd January 1935, a driver of Dulwich, London SE21, was arrested by Metropolitan Police Flying Squad officers and charged with receiving £518 of the mail train robbery money. This arrest calls for no further comment.

On 3rd October 1963 Douglas Gordon Goody, CRO 4290/46, born 11th March 1930, a hairdresser of Commondale, Putney, London SW15, was charged with two offences as follows:

(a) Conspiracy to stop a mail train with intent to rob, and
(b) Robbery.

The evidence against Goody was of a complicated nature and I will deal with some aspects of it. On 16th August 1963 a CID officer telephoned New Scotland Yard asking that Goody's home should be searched. This search was carried out by Flying Squad officers. Nothing of interest was found on the premises. Goody was not present and the search was carried out in the presence of his mother, with whom he lived. She said her son had left a few days before in a little red sports car and was either at Ramsgate or Margate.

On 22nd August 1963 Goody borrowed a Sunbeam Rapier car UUF 726 from the licensee of a London public house who had known Goody for 10 or 12 years. Goody had lived at the public house from time to time for the last three months. During the evening of 22nd August 1963 Goody arrived at the Grand Hotel, Leicester. He was in the company of a model from Oadby in Leicestershire. On the journey up to Leicester the Sunbeam Rapier car UUF 726 broke down at Cranfield, Bedfordshire. It was towed to a garage and Goody led the proprietor to believe it was his car and arranged for repairs to be carried out. He gave the name and address of the owner of the vehicle. He continued the journey to Leicester by taxi, where he went to the Grand Hotel and booked in under the same name and address. His actions in the Grand Hotel gave rise to suspicion and the Leicester City Police were informed.

Two CID officers of the Leicester City Police went to the Grand Hotel and saw the suspect. He persisted his name was that of the owner of the vehicle and finally they took him to police headquarters. He there admitted he was Goody and Aylesbury were informed.

At 3.15 p.m. on Friday 23rd August Goody was interviewed at Leicester City Police headquarters. He evaded replying to a question put to him about his movements at 3 a.m. 8th August 1963, the day of the robbery. He agreed it was the licensee's car he had used and that he had been living at the public house since his mother's house was searched. Finally he said 'Look I was away out of it, over the water on the Green Isle, so you can't fit me in.' He was asked if he meant he was in Ireland on 8th August 1963 and he replied 'Yes, I was there all the time and out of it.'

Goody was taken back to Aylesbury where he was interviewed by the head of the Flying Squad. Goody was again interviewed by this officer at 1 p.m. 24th August 1963 and denied he knew Leatherslade Farm. He was again interviewed at 11.45 p.m. 24th August and informed that as a result of enquiries made it was known that he travelled to Belfast by air on 2nd August 1963, with his mother and another man, but that he returned alone by air on 6th August 1963. Goody refused to say anything more. At 12.15 a.m. on 25th August 1963 Goody was released.

The model first met Goody in London in June 1963 when she was living in a flat in Putney. In turn Goody introduced her to two men. The second one, 'Bruce', she recognized as being one of the men circulated in the *Daily Telegraph* as wanted for the train robbery. This is undoubtedly Reynolds.

Between 17th and 20th July 1963 Goody told her that he was going to Ireland with his mother for a holiday. She did not wish him to write to her house so she gave him the address of a friend. On 9th August 1963 this friend delivered to her three postcards, all from Ireland and obviously from Goody. They were unfortunately destroyed by her before she was interviewed by the police. This friend when seen believed the postcards arrived at his address on Monday 5th August, Tuesday 6th August and Wednesday 7th August 1963.

Following the release of Goody on 25th August 1963 every effort was made to show exactly his movements on the vital days 6th to 9th August 1963.

When Goody was originally detained, a visit was made to the licensee of the public house by a Flying Squad officer and an expert from the forensic laboratory. They searched a room there which had been occupied by Goody. A pair of suede shoes was taken possession of from the wardrobe and the licensee identified them as Goody's property.

On the 14th August 1963 and on subsequent days when Leatherslade Farm was being examined and forensic and other samples taken, a squashed tin of yellow paint was noticed in a shed where the Austin lorry had been kept. It was not taken possession of at that time. Following an examination of Goody's shoes and the finding of yellow paint upon them this tin became significant. On the 28th August 1963 this tin was collected from the farm. The tin together with a sample of yellow paint from the lorry and a sample of yellow paint from the new land rover was taken to New Scotland Yard on 29th August 1963 and handed to the forensic laboratory. The vehicles were further examined on the 6th and 19th September 1963. On the 28th September further samples of yellow paint were taken from the garage floor at Leatherslade Farm.

Paint found in Goody's shoes was subsequently found to be identical in colour and chemical composition with samples of paint from the tin from Leatherslade Farm and from the vehicles found there. A jacket which was found at Boal's home was also examined and a knurled knob of yellow paint was found in the right jacket pocket. This paint was the same colour and chemical composition as that found on Goody's shoes. The forensic laboratory expert was quite satisfied that the shoes must have been at Leatherslade Farm. The coincidence of both the khaki and yellow paint being on one pair of shoes was far beyond reasonable assumption.

When arrested on 3rd October 1963 Goody admitted the shoes from the public house were his and that he had never lent them to anyone. On the instructions of his solicitor he refused to answer any more questions. The whole of the evidence against Goody was circumstantial and forensic.

On the 10th October 1963 Walter Albert Smith, CRO 2528/45, born 25th October 1930, a bookmaker's marker, was arrested. He was charged with receiving £2,000 in money between 2nd and 10th October 1963, the property of the Postmaster General. This arrest calls for no further comment.

On the evening of 25th October 1963 Robert Albert Welch, CRO 61730/58, born 12th March 1929, a club proprietor of Islington, London N1, was detained by Metropolitan Flying Squad officers. The following day he was charged at Aylesbury with:

(a) Conspiracy to stop a mail train with intent to rob it, and
(b) Robbery.

On the 14th August 1963 as a result of a message from

Aylesbury to New Scotland Yard, Flying Squad officers searched the home of Welch in London N1. He was not at home at the time although his wife was. Certain items of property were taken away by the officers and will be dealt with later.

On the 16th August 1963 Welch was seen by Flying Squad officers and questioned regarding his movements on the 7th and 8th August 1963. A written statement was taken. Among other things, Welch claimed that he had never been to Aylesbury or any of the surrounding towns.

On 25th October 1963 Welch was seen by Flying Squad officers in London. He was told that he would be taken to New Scotland Yard in connection with enquiries into the robbery at Cheddington, Buckinghamshire, in August of that year. Welch said, 'Do you mean the train job? I don't know anything about that, I don't even know Cheddington.' Welch was taken to New Scotland Yard where he was seen by the head of the Flying Squad. During the subsequent questioning, Welch denied knowing Leatherslade Farm, the area surrounding it or that part of the country at all. He also denied knowing Reynolds, James, Edwards and White, or any of the prisoners arrested at that time with the exception of Wisbey and Hussey.

Welch's finger and palm impressions were taken. These were compared with marks found at Leatherslade Farm. The palm impressions were found to be identical with marks on a 'Pipkin' can which had been left in a cupboard in the kitchen of Leatherslade Farm. At 3 p.m. 26th October 1963 Welch was taken to Aylesbury and charged.

The 'Pipkin' can on which the marks were found was one of nine found at the farm. Some were empty and some were full. This particular can was half full. It was found in the kitchen at Leatherslade Farm with two other full cans, each of which was stamped on top with a mauve number '723'. Of the other six cans,

Near the parish church of Aylesbury

four bear the same marking, but the other two cans were found on the bonfire and no marking could be seen on them because of the damage to them by fire. The beer which was filled into the cans at a brewery in Guildford on 23rd July 1963 had a short shelf life and thus stocks of it were dealt with in strict rotation.

Before the arrest of Welch, the town of Bicester in Oxfordshire had become a focal point in the enquiries. One of the gang believed Brian Field obtained the particulars of sale of Leatherslade Farm from an estate agent in that town. The town itself was within nine miles of Leatherslade Farm. During enquiries it was established that a man, who has never been identified, purchased on the 7th August 1963 ten cans of 'Pipkin' at an off-licence in Bicester. The off-licence manager obtained his supplies from Ind Coope (Oxford and West) Limited from their depot at Oxford on 1st August 1963; they in turn had received their supplies from the brewery at Guildford. Enquiries revealed that by 29th July 1963 Ind Coope had disposed of all their previous stocks of 'Pipkin' cans and that from 30th July 1963 they were distributing cans with the number '723' thereon. These particular cans were exhausted by 7th August 1963.

A 'Pipkin' can contains seven pints of beer and the Prosecution suggested that the purchase of 10 such cans must have been an unusual one. Further that the finding of nine cans at Leatherslade Farm, seven of which bore the same number as those sold at Bicester was proof that they were one and the same cans. This evidence was tendered at the Lower Court and was not challenged.

It was appreciated at that stage that much further enquiry would have to be made on this particular part of the evidence to combat any suggestion by Welch of innocent access to the one can of 'Pipkin'. It was found that to safely combat the alibi would need investigation of some 2,574 cans of 'Pipkin' which had been distributed to depots and retailers in the south of England.

In the first instance lists of retailers were obtained from the depots. A questionnaire was then drawn up and, together with a covering report outlining the facts, was sent to local police stations. Officers were asked to visit retailers situated in their district, get them to complete the questionnaire and, where any retailer had sold six or more cans at one time, obtain a statement relating to the customer who had made the purchase. This in turn, in some cases, had to be followed up by the customer being seen and asked to account for his disposal of the cans. The information received at Buckinghamshire headquarters was collated and sifted. Finally a complete schedule was prepared dealing with all the 'Pipkin' cans.

The Prosecution was then in a position to combat any suggestion by Welch of innocent access. It was thought that Welch would put forward a story that he had attended many parties at which 'Pipkin' cans were used and probably touched a can there. In reality he did not do this and merely put forward an innocent call at the farm after the robbery when he was offered beer from a 'Pipkin'. Many pieces of evidence often required exhaustive treatment and this has been included here as an example of one such case.

When Welch's home was searched on the 14th August, Flying Squad officers took possession of a paid hotel bill from a sideboard. It was for an amount of £19 7s. made chargeable to Mr Richards by the proprietors of a hotel in Nottingham. This was for accommodation for five men on the 22nd May 1963. Only one signed the register and gave his address as 35 Brompton Road, London (false).

It can be mentioned here that a mysterious male caller visited the estate agents in Bicester on 24th June 1963 in connection with the sale of Leatherslade Farm. He gave the name of Richards. Bicester of course is where the 'Pipkin' cans were sold.

When the hotel bill was examined for fingerprints a print identified as that of James Hussey was found on it. Subsequently the hotel receptionist picked out Hussey at an identification parade at Aylesbury as one of the five men who stayed at the hotel in Nottingham on the 22nd May 1963, a fact previously mentioned.

On the 2nd December 1963 all the prisoners arrested to date appeared before the Linslade magistrates sitting at Aylesbury. The Prosecution asked for the accused to be committed for trial on the charges which had been listed and produced to the court.

Compliments were then paid by the chairman to the Prosecuting Counsel and to the police for the competent way in which the case had been presented.

On 10th December 1963 Roy John James, CRO 17638/56, aged 28 years, born 30th August 1935, a silversmith of St John's Wood, London, was arrested by Flying Squad officers and charged with being concerned with others in committing the robbery.

At Leatherslade Farm the Fingerprint Department, New Scotland Yard, examined a blue-edged glass plate and a 'Johnson's' traveller's kit. On the plate and on the cellophane wrapping of the traveller's kit he developed some finger impressions which he identified as those of James.

On the 14th August 1963 35 mailbags were removed from Leatherslade Farm. These were taken to Buckinghamshire force headquarters at Aylesbury, emptied and the contents examined.

The mass of papers and paper scraps were sorted and put into nine mailbags which were delivered to New Scotland Yard on 16th August 1963, and handed to the Fingerprint Branch. On a loose page in an American magazine called *Movie Screen* finger impressions were developed and identified as those of James. It is of interest to mention here that on cellophane wrappers, in addition to the fingerprints of James, were found those of the prisoner Wilson.

Following upon the identification of James's fingerprints upon these articles, appeals were issued by the Press Bureau at New Scotland Yard on 23rd and 27th August 1963 to representatives of the press, radio and television to help in tracing him.

James's behaviour following the announcements that he was 'wanted' shows conclusively that he knew of them and that he did everything he could to avoid being traced by the police.

During August 1963 James was living in Chelsea, SW3. He also had a garage for his racing car in Battersea. Flying Squad officers visited these premises on 22nd August 1963. The flat was searched and although they did not find anything of evidential value they saw that it had been vacated in a hurry and had been empty for some days. Milk in the refrigerator had turned sour and was solid.

James was returning from Goodwood motor racing track on 22nd August 1963 when, according to his companion, at about 6 p.m. he heard the news on the radio that Wilson had been arrested. Later, the companion's house in Notting Hill was searched by Flying Squad officers, and a brown paper parcel containing £545 in £1 notes was found. These facts have been mentioned here only to show that James knew of the possibility of his arrest on 22nd August 1963 and from then on he was 'missing' from society.

Although the Austin Mini Cooper, number 293 DBD, known to belong to James, was taken possession of by police on 23rd August and taken to Chalk Farm police garage, no enquiry was made for it by James.

On 10th October 1963 COC10 Branch officers took possession of a Brabham Ford, Formula Junior racing car and tracks from a garage in Spicer Street, London SW11. The car which was the property of James was taken to Chalk Farm police garage. Although the racing car was in possession of the police for two months before James's arrest, he made no enquiries of police about it. The abandonment of home, cars and mode of living by James was sufficient to establish the fact that he knew that the police wanted to see him and that he was evading them.

On 10th December 1963 Flying Squad officers went to the house in St John's Wood, London NW8. The door was knocked but no one answered although there were obvious signs that someone was on the premises. The Flying Squad officers then forced an entrance and were just in time to see James disappearing through a fanlight window on to the roof. It was noticed he was carrying a bag or holdall. He was chased over the roofs and eventually jumped into the back garden of another house, where he was detained. He denied all knowledge of the holdall he had been carrying. James was known to the officers and asked to explain where he was on the night of 7/8th August 1963 when the mail train was robbed at Cheddington. He denied having been to Leatherslade Farm. He was arrested and cautioned. In the meantime the holdall had been found but James refused to say anything about it.

Later James was searched. In his personal possession was £131 10s. In the holdall was £12,041. The numbers of two £5 notes found in James's personal possession were J 69 500747 and J 94 284281. These notes were identified as two reported stolen. A piece of paper in the holdall carried by James showed amounts totalling £109,500 which is thought to be roughly one man's share of the loot.

On the 10th December 1963 at about 6.35 p.m., as a result of information, Flying Squad officers went to a kiosk at Great Dover Street, London SE1. They found two sacks containing bundles of money. It was examined by the Metropolitan Forensic Science Laboratory and the Fingerprint Branch. The sacks and debris were taken away for forensic examination, and the two top and two bottom notes of each bundle were removed for fingerprint examination. Notes to the value of £401 were taken away, and the remainder of the money was counted and examined by an employee of the National Provincial Bank Limited. He counted £46,844, which makes the total amount found in the sacks £47,245. When the notes were examined by the employee of the National Provincial Bank he abstracted 57 £5 Bank of England notes which were identified by their serial numbers as being part of the high-valued packets sent on the train by the Kirkcudbright and Dunoon branches of the National Commercial Bank of Scotland Limited.

The preliminary examination of the sacks and debris suggested that the money had been buried in the ground. No finger impressions were found upon the notes.

THE PROVING OF THE AMOUNT STOLEN

A list containing details of the stolen property was prepared by officers of the Investigation Branch, General Post Office. It showed that in all 636 packages containing £2,595,997 10s. had been stolen. It will be appreciated that to prove this loss strictly, and in accordance with the rules of evidence, over 1,000 witnesses would have had to be called to give evidence. This was impracticable and would have involved a tremendous waste of time, not only by the police but by the court and the public. It was decided that no specific amount of money should be stated in the robbery charge but that the stolen property should be shown as 120 mailbags.

Evidence was collated on suitable amounts totalling in all something over half a million pounds. A schedule was prepared to prove the theft of 155 high-valued packages, containing in all £681,180 10s.

The circulation of the crime, wanted persons and extent through all media

TELEX, WIRELESS AND TELEPHONE

In the early stages no records were made of the wireless and telephone messages from the Buckinghamshire control room; they were simply entered on the control room log. After examination of the message book kept in connection with the train robbery, it was found that the following messages were circulated.

10.33 a.m. 8th August 1963

To C9 New Scotland Yard, the chief constables of Berkshire, Oxfordshire, Northamptonshire, Bedfordshire and Hertfordshire.

> At approximately 0245 hours today a mail train robbery occurred between Leighton Buzzard and Cheddington, Bucks. 120 mailbags containing a very considerable sum of money are missing.
>
> It is thought that persons responsible may have hidden up and attempt to get away by mingling with normal morning traffic.
>
> Observation and frequent spot checks of traffic vehicles is requested.

9.30 a.m. 9th August 1963

To chief constables, Bedfordshire, Hertfordshire and Northamptonshire.

> Ref: Railway Robbery
> Bearing in mind possibility that the stolen mailbags might still be concealed within a reasonable distance of Cheddington, would you please continue the searches you have already organized of

Posters on a police notice board – one offering a £10,000 reward by the Buckinghamshire Constabulary for information regarding the robbery

derelict farm buildings, barns, disused railway bridges, canal barges and other likely places. In addition to mailbags we are interested in a 10-ton army lorry and a light blue or grey long wheel base land rover with a hard top. One of these vehicles may have a broken wing mirror.

Action Copy this to all divisions with addendum. Similar searches to be made throughout Buckinghamshire.

9.27 p.m. 11th August 1963

From New Scotland Yard and Buckinghamshire Constabulary to the chief constables of Bedfordshire, Oxfordshire, Oxford City, Berkshire, Northamptonshire, Northampton Borough, Hertfordshire and New Scotland Yard and to all divisions of Buckinghamshire.

Re: Rail Robbery
Attention of all foot and mobile patrols is drawn to the fact that the money may be moved at night either in bulk or in part.

10 p.m. 12th August 1963

To all divisions in Buckinghamshire, the chief constables of Hertfordshire, Bedfordshire and Northamptonshire.

Reference to mail robbery
Bearing in mind that premises might have been specifically purchased or rented for use for the immediate concealment of the stolen property and its transport, please have enquiries made of estate agents and obtain information of transactions during the past six months involving likely premises within 30 miles of Cheddington, particularly farms, derelict houses, etc. Please follow up where appropriate.

EXPRESS MESSAGES AND MESSAGES IN CONNECTION WITH THESE

In all 19 express messages or messages in connection with same were circulated. These can be summarized as follows:

5.36 p.m. 9th August 1963 to all Districts No. 52/63.
Attention to the 10-ton army trucks.

8.46 p.m. 10th August 1963 to all Districts No. 53/63.
Attention to two vehicles seen near Cheddington.

12.01 a.m. 13th August 1963 to 5 and 6 Districts No. 55/63.
Relating to a Commer Van.

2.30 a.m. 13th August 1963 to 5 and 6 Districts No. 56/63.
Further information re Commer Van and attention to caravan sites.

5.46 p.m. 13th August 1963 to all Districts No. 57/63.
Cancelling express message 52/63.

11.35 p.m. 17th August 1963 For circulation to 4, 5, 6, 7 and 8.
This is similar to express message 60/63 and apparently made the subject of express message 60/63.

1.20 a.m. 18th August 1963 to Districts 4, 5, 6, 7 and 8 No. 60/63.
Reference person calling at garage in London with Austin Healey sports car 222 NFC.

11.58 p.m. 18th August 1963 to Districts 4, 5, 6, 7 and 8 63/63.
Cancellation of previous two messages in so far as it relates to 222 NFC – recovered.

1.36 p.m. 22nd August 1963 to all Districts and all Ports 66/63.
Train robbery at Cheddington, Buckinghamshire, 8th August
when approximately 2 ¼ million pounds stolen. Wanted for
participation in this offence – Reynolds, Wilson, White.

4.13 p.m. 22nd August 1963 to all Districts and all Ports 67/63.
Cancel 66/63 so far as Wilson concerned, arrested.

7.01 p.m. 23rd August 1963 to all Districts 69/63.
Roy John James wanted and car 293 DBD.

1.24 p.m. 11th December 1963
Ordinary telephone message, notifying Divisions and Oxford
County of arrest of James and that express message 69/63 would
be cancelled in Gazettes.

1.59 p.m. 24th August 1963 to all Districts and Ports Warning 70/63.
To amend express message 69/63.

6.14 p.m. 24th August 1963 to all Districts and Ports Warning 71/63.
Further to express messages 69 and 70/63. Car found.

7.40 p.m. 27th August 1963 to all Districts and all Ports 72/63.
Reynolds believed in possession of car BMK 723A.

5.25 p.m. 13th September 1963 to all Districts 78/63.
Attention called to red Morris 480 GLM.

7.47 p.m. 13th September 1963 to all Districts 80/63.
Attention to Ronald Edwards.

8.47 p.m. 13th September 1963 to all Districts 81/63.

Cancel 78/63. Car located.

LOCAL CRIME INFORMATIONS

The only crime informations traced, and there is no reason to believe there are others, are as follows:

(a) 20th August 1963. Letter to the force to the effect that the train was robbed at Sears Crossing, Buckinghamshire, on 8th August and that a large amount of money comprising £1 and £5 notes stolen. A possibility that some of the money had been deposited in derelict or unused buildings in the county and requesting a search be made. If anything found, not to be touched but Buckinghamshire headquarters informed at once.

(b) 13th September 1963. Particulars of persons police were anxious to trace in connection with the train robbery. These were Ronald Edwards, Roy John James, Bruce Richard Reynolds, James Edward White and a woman known as 'Sheree' White. Composite of circulations made in *Police Gazette*, commencing 22nd August 1963.

(c) A circular letter undated asking that enquiries be made at supermarkets and multiple stores in a 30-mile radius of Aylesbury to trace any bulk buying (a dozen or more of each item) of foodstuffs – described – between 25th July and 10th August 1963.

(d) Booklet published on 17th December 1963 by Buckingham-shire Constabulary of which 1,000 were printed and circulated to all chief constables in England, Wales, Scotland and the Channel Islands. This contained photographs and descriptions of Ronald Edwards, Bruce Richard Reynolds, James Edward White (and a woman he was associating with, Sheree White). This booklet was produced in a handy size for convenient carrying in a notebook pocket.

The *Police Gazette* carried the following circulations in connection with the train robbery.

(a) On the 22nd August the first circulation appeared which gave a general account of the robbery, the amount of money thought to have been stolen at that time and particulars of persons in custody at that time.

(b) *Police Gazettes* of 23rd, 24th and 25th August showed particulars of persons wanted.

(c) The *Police Gazette* of 26th August carried a five-page special supplement, giving the numbers of £5 notes known to have been stolen.

(d) *Police Gazettes* of 28th and 30th August gave particulars of further persons wanted.

(e) The *Police Gazette* of 6th September 1963 carried a seven-page special supplement giving amended numbers of notes stolen and cancelling the special supplement of the 26th August. The numbers of the stolen notes had been obtained by the GPO as conveyers of the stolen money from the banks concerned.

(f) The *Police Gazette* of Thursday 12th September gave particulars of further persons wanted.

(g) *Police Gazette* of 28th September included a poster showing persons whose whereabouts were being sought for the robbery. Forces were asked to place the poster at police stations where it could be seen by members of the public. Approximately 9,000 posters were dispatched. The poster was so worded that anyone seeing and reading it could have little doubt that the police wished to interview the persons whose photographs and names appeared on it.

(h) *Police Gazettes* of 6th December 1963 and 9th December 1963 showed persons arrested.

THE GENERAL POST OFFICE

The Public Relations Department of the Post Office Headquarters, London EC1, authorized the publication, issue and distribution of posters for display in post offices throughout the United Kingdom. On the 8th October 1963, 25,436 copies of a poster, prepared from the police poster and almost a duplicate of it, were printed. These were distributed to head and district post-masters throughout the United Kingdom for re-distribution to all post offices under their control and for display at the post offices.

PRESS, RADIO AND TELEVISION APPEALS

Following upon the identification of the five wanted men from fingerprints found at Leatherslade Farm, the Press Bureau of New Scotland Yard issued appeals to representatives of the press, radio and television to help in tracing them. The dates of these with the subjects to whom they relate are shown below:

(a) 22nd August 1963 – Reynolds and White
(b) 23rd August 1963 – James
(c) 27th August 1963 – Reynolds and James
(d) 28th August 1963 – White
(e) 30th August 1963 – Reynolds
(f) 12th September 1963 – Edwards
(g) 6th October 1963 – Edwards

The appeals appeared in all the leading daily and Sunday news-papers and the *London Evening Standard*.

On the British Broadcasting Corporation Home Service news

bulletin 50 announcements were made and on the Light Programme 76 announcements were made in news bulletins and summaries. On the British Broadcasting Corporation television news photographs etc. of wanted persons appeared on 30 occasions. Independent Television News Limited transmitted information and photographs of the persons wanted on 32 occasions. As a result of the appeals made through all three media a flood of information was received.

Letters were received from representatives of the press, radio and television showing to what extent news relating to the wanted men was circulated and the name of their representative who could, if necessary, give evidence of particulars of their publications.

Police investigating the scene of the robbery

The work of Scotland Yard

The initial report from the Cheddington signal box which spoke of a break-in at Cheddington Railway Station was received in the railway control room at Euston. They in turn passed the message to New Scotland Yard, at 4.24 a.m. 8th August 1963, who notified Buckinghamshire Constabulary headquarters at 4.25 a.m. The text of the message, having regard to its content, could hardly be expected to arouse other than normal police action in such circumstances.

The commander (Crime), New Scotland Yard, gained first information of the train robbery by way of newspaper reports and wireless broadcasts on the morning of 8th August 1963. The first message relating to the robbery was sent to COC9 New Scotland Yard by telex at 10.33 a.m. 8th August 1963. During that morning the commander received a telephone call from the chief constable of Buckinghamshire, who informed him of the robbery and asked that New Scotland Yard be represented at a meeting of the General Post Office and other organizations involved, to be held at 3 p.m. that afternoon, at the headquarters of the General Post Office, St Martins-le-Grand, London. The commander attended the meeting accompanied by the second in command of COC8 (the Flying Squad) and the detective superintendent of COC1.

At the meeting the head of the Buckinghamshire Constabulary outlined the facts surrounding the 'train robbery' as known at that time. A discussion took place and the commander suggested that this was undoubtedly a crime planned in London by London criminals – it having occurred in Buckinghamshire being incidental. A further point made by the commander, particularly in view of the remark made by one of the robbers to the fireman on the train, that he was not to move for half an hour, was that the robbers may well have hidden with their 'booty' within half an hour's travelling distance from the scene of the attack. He estimated this distance as between 25 and 30 miles and suggested that a systemized search and roadblocks should be organized, assuming of course that something of the sort was already in hand and would be extended following the meeting. Particular emphasis was made that the searchers should concentrate on isolated farms and buildings. (No minutes were taken of the meeting which would verify the suggestions attributed to the commander, and they were not remembered by other persons present.)

At the conclusion of the meeting it was arranged by the commander that the detective superintendent of COC1 and a detective sergeant would travel to Aylesbury that day to assist and advise the Buckinghamshire Police in the investigation.

During the days following the robbery, the commander received a number of calls from various chief constables asking when further information concerning the robbery would be circulated. He, too, was disturbed at the lack of circulation and telephoned Aylesbury on Friday 9th, Saturday 10th, Sunday 11th and Monday 12th August, and requested progress reports and anything of value for circulation. Not being satisfied with the progress he expressed his concern to the deputy commander and together with him travelled to Aylesbury on the 13th August 1963 and spent two hours discussing the situation. Whilst he was there Leatherslade Farm, the hideout of the robbers, was discovered. The commander visited the farm and personally made the arrangements respecting the guarding of it until the arrival of the fingerprint and forensic experts. Having no method of communication from the farm, he together with other senior officers visited Brill Police Station, where he again personally telephoned New Scotland Yard and made the necessary arrangements for the 'experts' to attend.

The commander then returned to Aylesbury and further arranged for a detective inspector, two detective sergeants and a detective constable of the Metropolitan Police to attend at Aylesbury to take over the administration and organization of the train robbery incident room, as he considered it was not functioning as smoothly as it should have been. This was not meant as a reflection on the officers already in the incident room, who were dealing with a vast amount of work, but merely to strengthen the administrative side, so vital when investigations are being carried out into a crime of this magnitude. It was at this time too that the detective superintendent of COC1 was made responsible primarily for the progressing of reports and paper work, and the detective chief superintendent of No. 1 District Metropolitan Police (later in charge of Flying Squad), was placed in overall charge of the train robbery investigation. A detective sergeant in each district of the Metropolitan Police was given the specific job of liaison officer for the train robbery enquiries.

One other matter which gave grave concern to the commander was that the press seemed to have far too much sway at Aylesbury. They appeared to be wandering about all over the headquarters building and advance publicity was getting into the press about police moves and lines of action. To counteract this he gave certain instructions as to the handling of the press at the London end of the enquiry and to some extent at Aylesbury. For this reason little information of the London end of the enquiry was passed to Aylesbury; it was considered sufficient to pass on the prisoners to them as they were arrested and the evidence connecting them with the robbery.

The *Police Gazette* publication on 22nd August 1963, giving particulars of the crime, persons in custody and specific lines of enquiry to be followed, was formulated by the commander himself.

Certain information was received by the commander giving the names of 15 criminals who were either directly or indirectly concerned with the robbery. This information was passed on to those in charge of the investigation. Suffice it to say that from the time the crime was committed to the termination of the trials, the commander gave the crime his personal attention.

THE FLYING SQUAD

Prior to the meeting held at 3 p.m. on 8th August 1963 at the General Post Office, London, a detective inspector was re-allocated from another case to which he had been put the previous day to deal exclusively with enquiries directed to the Flying Squad and/or divisions concerning the mail train robbery. An incident room was set up for the squad and manned by two officers who were responsible for collating, logging and seeing that attention was given to all information received.

In the weeks that followed the robbery at least 18 Flying Squad officers and often as many as 30 worked exclusively on the case. During this time teams put in a minimum of 18 hours per day per man. There was a directive that no matter what enquiries officers or teams had in hand they were at all times to give priority to the train robbery enquiries. There was also a daily liaison with the effort COC1 were making.

Between the 8th August and 28th August 1963, on which date the incident room at New Scotland Yard closed down, 1,651 messages were received, many of which required specific lines of action. These were systematically cross-indexed each with the other and alphabetically. From the 9th August 1963 to 30th September 1963, 419 searches of premises were made, many in connection with the train robbery. For the same period of 1962 the Flying Squad carried out only 188 searches which shows the extent of effort. This effort led to a number of arrests not connected with the train robbery. At one place raided the printing of forged £5 notes was in full swing and at another a large amount of electrical goods stolen by means of warehouse-breaking was recovered. A number of arrests resulted. One very interesting point revealed itself as the enquiry and searches in London gathered momentum, that *serious crime virtually stood still because of the tremendous increase in Criminal Investigation Department activity*.

The number of arrests made by the Flying Squad and Metropolitan Police in connection with the train robbery, all of which have been covered earlier in the report, totalled 19.

FINGERPRINT BRANCH (C3)

On the 9th August 1963, a request was received by the detective chief superintendent of COC3, New Scotland Yard, from the detective superintendent of COC1, for fingerprint officers to examine the diesel engine and the first two coaches of the attacked mail train. Accordingly a detective superintendent, two detective inspectors and a photographer went to Cheddington on the 10th August and spent the day there making their examination. The train and coaches yielded nothing from the point of view of evidence, but the movement of the diesel engine and parcels van prior to the examination had meant a good deal of additional enquiries and comparisons to enable marks found to be eliminated.

On the 13th August 1963, following the discovery of Leatherslade Farm, a request was again made from Aylesbury for fingerprint staff to visit there to examine the scene of crime. On that day the same fingerprint officers went to Leatherslade Farm and remained at the scene until the examination was complete, which was four days later. The fact that an adequate guard had been put on the farm, thus denying access to everyone until the fingerprint examination was complete, proved invaluable when fingerprint evidence was given at the trial. The total number of

photographs of sets of fingerprints taken there was 243, which included 311 fingers and 56 bits of palms. As each print was discovered the head fingerprint officer was called and he would develop it himself. This was vital when he gave the fingerprint evidence at the trial as he is one of the few experts prepared to discuss the age of a print in the witness box. By being able to give the evidence relating to the development of the print he was able to discuss the 'reasons' behind statements of age.

One particular instance where the age of a print played an important part was in the case of Hussey, whose palm print was discovered on the tailboard of a lorry used to transport the stolen money and found at Leatherslade Farm. The defence endeavoured to show that this had been legitimately transposed when Hussey was asked to assist in the delivery of some greengrocery to Leatherslade Farm. This was rebutted when the age of that particular mark was put at more than four days from the time at which he found it.

On completion of the work at the farm 1,534 bank envelopes and a number of newspapers found at the farm together with other loose items were removed to New Scotland Yard. A room was set aside there to deal specifically with the mail train robbery and a telephone was installed. A team of four civilian searchers and the two detective inspectors who went to Leatherslade Farm dealt exclusively with the scene of crime marks found. With regard to the 1,534 bank envelopes etc., two men in the Fingerprint Branch, overlooked by a sergeant 1st class, were used to process, dry heat and examine these documents for fingerprints.

Further searches were also made by the Fingerprint Branch at two addresses in London and of the caravan found in Surrey. The names of 164 suspects were put forward for search and 793 sets of elimination prints were taken. It was estimated in the Fingerprint

Checking fingerprints at New Scotland Yard

Branch that in the region of 750,000 comparisons were made. Early on during the enquiry the commander put forward a list of 17 suspects which included, as it turned out, the names of seven persons who were connected with the train robbery.

The Fingerprint Branch at New Scotland Yard worked until Christmas 1963 exclusively on the mail train robbery. A detective inspector in the branch was made responsible for schedules and for keeping records of prints found on articles and producing these exhibits at the trial. As all arrests have not yet been made a number of Fingerprint Branch staff are still partly engaged on checking prints etc. against suspects.

Of the persons arrested, seven were identified by means of fingerprints found at Leatherslade Farm and two by fingerprints found elsewhere. Of the persons still wanted, two have been identified by fingerprints found at Leatherslade Farm and one by fingerprints found elsewhere.

When the cases containing money were found in Surrey, they were examined for fingerprints by Surrey Constabulary officers. Thirteen marks in all were found and photographed; five of these photographs of fingerprints which were considered to contain sufficient detail for identification and production in court were eventually forwarded to New Scotland Yard and identified as those of Brian Arthur Field. The remaining eight photographs were called for and yielded a number of prints, which although not sufficient for production in court were brought out in cross-examination as belonging to Brian Arthur Field, which considerably strengthened the case against him.

CRIMINAL INTELLIGENCE COC11

On the 8th August 1963 a report submitted by the detective superintendent in charge of the branch put forward the names of four men, as a result of information received, who may have been concerned with the train robbery. One of them was Robert Albert Welch, CRO 61730/58, who was subsequently arrested and convicted.

On the 13th August 1963 a number of nicknames were supplied to the branch with the request that they be identified. From the records examined in the branch a number of names were put forward which included:

Douglas G. Goody   CRO 4290/46
Roy J. James   CRO 17638/56
Bruce R. Reynolds   CRO 41212/48
Charles Frederick Wilson CRO 5010/54

All these men were arrested in connection with the train robbery with the exception of Bruce Richard Reynolds, who is still wanted.

On 10th August 1963 information was received that a farm about 20 minutes run, and off the road, from Aylesbury was being used as a hideout by the thieves and should be searched within 48 hours. The occupier was believed to be a horse dealer. This information was considered of such importance that two senior officers went to Aylesbury at once, arriving there at 12.30 a.m. 11th August 1963, where they conferred with the detective superintendent of COC1. This information led to the searches made on Sunday 11th August 1963.

On the 28th August the branch identified a man known as 'Buster' as Ronald Christopher Edwards, CRO 33533/61. This man is still wanted.

On the 3rd December 1963 it was reported that as a result of three weeks' enquiries and observations by officers of the branch, it was certain that one of the men who was wanted for the train robbery was living with his wife in a flat in Eaton Square, London SW1. This information was passed on to those in charge and at 4 p.m. that day the person was arrested. (He was subsequently acquitted.)

CRIMINAL RECORD OFFICE COC4

This department supplied to Aylesbury a large number of criminal records. At no time was there any delay in forwarding these records to Aylesbury on request and searches of records were always made immediately.

FRAUD SQUAD COC6

After the discovery of Leatherslade Farm it became apparent that the enquiries respecting the sale of the farm would be prolonged and difficult, particularly as it involved John Denby Wheater, solicitor, Brian Arthur Field, solicitors managing clerk, and Leonard Denis Field. A detective chief inspector of the Fraud Squad with expert knowledge of conveyancing was put in charge of this aspect of the investigation. It was entirely due to the enquiries made by him that Wheater was arrested and charged.

THE STOLEN MOTOR VEHICLE SQUAD COC10

When Leatherslade Farm was discovered and the three vehicles used on the robbery were found there, a detective chief inspector and a vehicle examiner from the department visited the farm and thoroughly examined the vehicles. As a result of their examination, and in a very short time, the complete history of each vehicle was compiled. Two were found to have been purchased and the other one stolen. This enquiry connects very definitely with the robbery James Edward White, CRO 26113/35, who is still wanted.

THE METROPOLITAN POLICE FORENSIC SCIENCE LABORATORY

The laboratory played a very important part from the very first day. The scene of the attack on the mail train was visited by a senior staff member and a detective inspector, who remained for three days. Following the discovery of Leatherslade Farm, the same two officials, a detective chief inspector and four laboratory staff attended. The majority of this staff remained at Aylesbury for three days, collecting, sorting, logging and removing exhibits. In some cases immediate examination was made in a room set aside for laboratory staff at Buckinghamshire County police headquarters. After initial examination, those items for further examination were passed to the Metropolitan Police laboratory.

Between 200 and 300 mailbags and over 1,000 other items were examined and rejected. Visits were made by the laboratory staff in company with Flying Squad officers to the homes of 14 suspects. This was invaluable in the case of Goody. Three hundred and twenty-five actual forensic exhibits, some of which were divided into as many as six sub-exhibits, were produced at the trial.

The press

Immediately the news of the train robbery became known the Buckinghamshire Constabulary headquarters at Aylesbury was inundated with telephone calls from the press. On the first day telephone lines urgently required for the conduct of police business were continually blocked by incoming press calls and this continued despite extra lines being installed by the General Post Office. Press interference developed to such an extent that reporters had the habit of wandering over the headquarters building at Aylesbury, and finding their way into offices where confidential matters were being dealt with. Investigating officers were continually pursued whilst making enquiries and often matters appeared in the press which could only hamper enquiries. This state of affairs persisted until the detective chief superintendent of No. 1 District Metropolitan Police was placed in overall charge of the investigation, when he restricted their activities. Often information appeared in the press of enquiries being made respecting suspects in London. This position resulted in matters of importance not being freely discussed between investigating officers for fear of information being inadvertently leaked to the press. This state of affairs no doubt resulted in Aylesbury not getting information of pending arrests and not knowing of them until the prisoners arrived there.

The assistance of the press was called on in a number of instances to publish particulars of persons the police wished to trace, and they played their part in this direction to the full. This aspect of press cooperation was commented on earlier.

On the days which followed the robbery all the national press covered the train robbery to the full. Generally speaking early press comment was sympathetic to the problems involved in

investigating the crime and dealt mainly with reconstructing the robbery, injuries to the train crew and the likely methods by which the monies could be disposed of by the thieves. Later reports showed sustained police activity, the rewards offered by the assessors and appeals to the public for help, particularly in relation to the type of premises likely to be used by the thieves as a hideout. Many pieces of information came to light as a result, not least amongst them the message from the herdsman respecting Leatherslade Farm.

The *Guardian* of the 16th August 1963 published an article under the heading 'Textbook example of modern investigation. Police flexibility and speed'. This was a good pointer to responsible press opinion. On the 21st August 1963 *The Times* published an article under the heading 'Test Case'. Attention was drawn to the fact that the mail train robbery had not unnaturally unleashed strong demands for the establishment of a national Criminal Investigation Department. It went on to say that such demands were not unreasonable, but they had to be examined with caution. The article concluded by saying that if the CID could demonstrate that as at present organized they could recover most of the money and bring the real offenders to book fairly speedily, the upholders of the present system would have won the right to maintain that it is best to leave well alone. If they failed, it could only be concluded that radical re-appraisals are necessary.

Front-page news in the *Daily Herald* of 17th April 1964 had the headlines 'Did the Yard blunder? Desk men hindered train raid hunt'. This accused Scotland Yard chiefs in control of policy and administration of being 50 years behind the times. It suggested that at least half the people who conspired to rob the mail train were still free and that time and time again detectives were not allowed to make moves they considered vital. Instead they had to carry out the orders of 'armchair policemen', who some detectives claimed were out of touch with modern criminal methods. It claimed that the worst administrative errors were in the lack of coordination at the Yard and failure to appreciate the value of the right publicity at the right time. The article further went on to say that many times the Flying Squad were working in London without information being passed back to officers in charge of the investigation at Aylesbury.

STORY OF THE ROBBERY TO THE PRESS

The enquiry into the investigation of the train robbery and lessons to be learned from this was commenced on the 8th April 1964. On that date the detective superintendent in charge of this enquiry stated in the chief constable's office at Aylesbury, in the presence of the chief constable and one of Her Majesty's Inspectors of Constabulary, that he had written an article on the train robbery of between 50 and 60,000 words and had handed the script to the *Sunday Telegraph*. The edited version was subsequently published in the *Sunday Telegraph* in two instalments, the first on the 19th April and the second on the 26th April 1964.

This officer joined the Buckinghamshire Constabulary on the 9th March 1931 and retired from that force on the 11th April 1964. He handed in his notice of resignation on 16th March 1964. It will thus be seen that at the time of writing the article he was a serving police officer.

The verdicts and sentences

Prison sentences were passed on 16/17 April 1964. Where applicable, the following includes the judge's address to the prisoner before sentence.

ROGER JOHN CORDREY
Trial commenced: 20 January 1964
Date of conviction: 20 January 1964 (pleaded guilty)

> You are the first to be sentenced out of certainly 11 greedy men whom hope of gain allured. You and your co-accused have been convicted of complicity in one way or another in a crime which in its impudence and enormity is the first of its kind in this country. I propose to do all in my power to ensure it will also be the last of its kind. For your outrageous conduct constitutes an intolerable menace to the well-being of society. Let us clear out of the way any romantic notion of dare-devilry; this is nothing less than a sordid crime of violence inspired by vast greed. All who have seen that nerve-shattered engine driver can have no doubt of the nerve-racking affect on the law-abiding citizens of a concerted assault by armed robbers.
>
> To deal with this case leniently would be a positively evil thing. When grave crime is committed it calls for grave punishment, not for the purpose of mere retribution but that others similarly tempted will be brought to the realization that crime does not pay and the game is not worth even the most alluring candle.
>
> Potential criminals who might be dazzled by the enormity of the prize must be taught that the punishment they risk will be

proportionately greater. I therefore find myself with the unenviable duty of pronouncing grave sentences. You and the other accused vary widely in intelligence, strength of personality and antecedent history and other ways. Some of you have absolutely clean characters up to the present. Some have previous convictions of a comparatively minor character. Others have previous convictions of gravity which could lead to sentences of corrective training or preventive detention. To some the degradation to which you have all now sunk will bring consequences vastly more cruel than to others. Whatever the past of a particular accused, it pales into insignificance in the light of his present offences. Furthermore, the evidence, or rather the lack of it, renders it impossible to determine exactly what part was played by each of the 11 accused convicted of the larger conspiracy or the eight convicted of actual robbery. I therefore propose after mature deliberation to treat you all in the same manner with two exceptions.

You, Cordrey, are the first of the exceptions. When arrested you immediately gave information to police which enabled them to put their hands on nearly £80,000 and the remainder was eventually recovered. Furthermore, at the outset of this trial you confessed your guilt and I feel I should give recognition to that fact. I do this because it is greatly in the public interest that the guilty should confess their guilt. This massive trial is the best demonstration of the truth of that proposition.

Cordrey was sentenced to 20 years for conspiracy to rob; 20 years for receiving £56,037; 20 years for receiving £79,120; 20 years for receiving £5,060 (concurrent). He was found not guilty of robbery.

RONALD ARTHUR BIGGS
Trial commenced: 8 April 1964
Date of conviction: 15 April 1964

> Yesterday you were convicted on both the first and second counts of this indictment. Your learned Counsel has urged that you had no special talent and you were plainly not an originator of the conspiracy. Those submissions I bear in mind. I do not know when you entered the conspiracy or what part you played. What I do know is that you are a specious and facile liar and you have this week perjured yourself time and again.

Biggs was sentenced to 25 years for conspiracy to rob and 30 years for robbery (concurrent).

WILLIAM GERALD BOAL
Trial commenced: 20 January 1964
Date of conviction: 26 March 1964

> You, substantially the eldest of the accused, have been convicted of conspiracy to rob a mail and of armed robbery. You have expressed no repentance for your wrongdoing. Instead you continue to assert your innocence but you beg for mercy. I propose to extend to you some measure of mercy. I do this on account of your age and because having seen and heard you I cannot believe that you were one of the originators of the conspiracy or that you played a very dynamic part in it or the robbery itself. Your participation in any degree, nevertheless, remains a matter of extreme gravity.

Boal was sentenced to 21 years for conspiracy to rob and 24 years for robbery (concurrent). The jury was discharged from giving

Three of the robbers leaving court at Linslade

verdict on three counts: receiving £78,982, receiving £56,047; receiving £5,910.

BRIAN ARTHUR FIELD
Trial commenced: 20 January 1964
Date of conviction: 26 March 1964

You have been convicted on counts 1 and 12 of conspiring to rob a mail and conspiracy to obstruct the course of justice. Of the right of both these verdicts I personally entertain no doubt whatever. By native ability, of no mean kind, and by hard work, you attained the responsible position of solicitor's managing clerk. Your strength of personality and superior intelligence enabled you, I strongly suspect, to obtain a position of dominance in relation to your employer John Wheater. I entertain no serious doubts that you are in no small measure responsible for the disastrous position in which this wretched man now finds himself.

You are one of the very few convicted persons in this trial of whom it can be said with any degree of certainty what it was you were able to contribute to the furtherance of crime. Whether it was a product of your mind or of Leonard Field or of some other entirely different person that originated the idea of acquiring the possession of Leatherslade Farm with the subterfuge that it was wanted for purely honest means, I have no way of knowing. Whether it was simply a remarkable coincidence that two of the bags found in the Dorking woods were yours or whether they might have been evidence of your duplicity I have no means of knowing, but I accept the jury's verdict. That you played an essential role in the major conspiracy is clear. Out of that there naturally flowed the later conspiracy to obstruct justice. I have borne in mind your antecedents, etc. You expressed regret for the position in which you now find yourself. That is understandable.

Brian Field was sentenced to 25 years for conspiracy to rob and 5 years for conspiracy to obstruct justice (concurrent). He was found not guilty of robbery and of receiving £100,900.

LEONARD DENIS FIELD

Trial commenced: 20 January 1964
Date of conviction: 26 March 1964

> Although you have but one previous conviction, which I ignore, you are a dangerous man. Not only have you perjured yourself repeatedly in this trial to save your own skin, but on your own showing at one stage you perjured yourself in an endeavour to ruin the accused Brian Field.
>
> I sentence you not for perjury; I sentence you solely for conspiracy. The overt act committed by you in pursuance of that conspiracy is beyond doubt. You made a vital contribution. Once having joined the major conspiracy, the lesser conspiracy to obstruct justice was a natural outcome. I bear in mind your antecedent history and those other matters urged on me by your Counsel.

Leonard Field was sentenced to 25 years for conspiracy to rob and 5 years for conspiracy to obstruct justice (concurrent). The jury was discharged from giving verdict on the count of robbery.

DOUGLAS GORDON GOODY

Trial commenced: 20 January 1964
Date of conviction: 26 March 1964

> You have been convicted on the first and second counts of this indictment. You have a bad record, notably with a conviction for

grave violence at the early age of 18. You qualify for preventive detention. Yet in some respects you present one of the saddest problems in this trial. For you have manifest gifts of personality and intelligence which could have carried you far had they been directed honestly. I have not seen you in this court for three months without noticing signs that you are a man capable of inspiring the admiration of your fellow accused. You have become a dangerous menace to society.

The Crown have said they don't consider this criminal enterprise was the product of any mastermind. I don't know that I necessarily agree with the Crown in that respect and I strongly suspect you played a major role both in the conspiracy and the robbery. Suspicion, however, is not good enough for me anymore than it would be for a jury. It would, therefore, be quite wrong for me to cause my suspicion to lead me to impose any heavier sentence on you than on the other accused.

Goody was sentenced to 25 years for conspiracy to rob and 30 years for robbery (concurrent).

MARTIN HARVEY
Trial commenced: 17 April 1964
Date of conviction: 17 April 1964 (pleaded guilty)
Harvey was sentenced to 12 months' imprisonment for receiving £518.

JAMES HUSSEY
Trial commenced: 20 January 1964
Date of conviction: 26 March 1964

You have previously been convicted of grave crimes including two involving violence. On the other hand, I accept that as a son

you are warm hearted. It is obvious you have qualities of personality and intelligence which you have put to very good stead in
this case.

Hussey was sentenced to 25 years for conspiracy to rob and 30
years for robbery (concurrent).

ROY JOHN JAMES
Trial commenced: 20 January 1964
Date of conviction: 26 March 1964

You are the only one out of all the accused in respect of whom it
has been proved you actually received a substantial part of the
stolen money. You still had £12,000 in your possession, and I have
no doubt that the original sum far exceeded that figure. Your
record in the past is a bad one. Corrective training seems to have
done you little or no good; yet you have ability of a kind which
would have assured you of an honest livelihood of substantial
proportion, for in a very short space of time you had what your
Counsel described as brilliant and meteoric success as a racing
driver.

I strongly suspect it was your known talent as a driver which
enabled you to play an important part in the perpetration of this
grave crime. It may be that you have never personally resorted to
physical violence. You have told me you went to Leatherslade
Farm knowing you were doing wrong; that you became
involved, but not in the robbery, and then ran away. I don't find it
possible to differentiate your case from most of the other
accused.

James was sentenced to 25 years for conspiracy to rob and 30 years
for robbery (concurrent). The jury was discharged from giving

urged on your behalf, but my duty as I see it is clear.

If you, or any of the other accused still to be dealt with, had assisted justice that would have told strongly in your favour. The consequence of this outrageous crime is that the vast booty of something like £2,500,000 still remains almost entirely unrecovered. It would be an affront to the public if anyone of you should be at liberty in anything like the near future to enjoy those ill-gotten gains.

Wilson was sentenced to 25 years for conspiracy to rob and 30 years for robbery (concurrent).

THOMAS WILLIAM WISBEY
Trial commenced: 20 January 1964
Date of conviction: 26 March 1964

You stand convicted on the first and second counts. Your previous record qualifies you for corrective training. But any such sentence is plainly out of the question. In your case again I have no evidence on which I can measure the degree or quality of your participation in the vast criminal enterprise which has given rise to this trial. Your Counsel has urged you are plainly not a dominant character and the part you played was subsidiary and was perhaps connected with transport matters. You yourself have thrown no light on that or any other topic. You have not sought to mollify the court by any repentance.

Wisbey was sentenced to 25 years for conspiracy to rob and 30 years for robbery (concurrent).

The train robbery appeals

The appeals commenced on Monday 6th July 1964 in the Court of Criminal Appeal, the Law Courts, London. The first appeals against conviction and sentence were those of:

(a) Roy John James, sentenced to 30 years' imprisonment.
(b) Charles Wilson, sentenced to 30 years' imprisonment.
(c) Ronald Arthur Biggs, sentenced to 30 years' imprisonment.
(d) James Hussey, sentenced to 30 years' imprisonment.
(e) Thomas William Wisbey, sentenced to 30 years' imprisonment.
(f) Robert Welch, sentenced to 30 years' imprisonment.

All the above-named appeared at the Court of Criminal Appeal with the exception of Wilson, who remained in prison.

When discussing the appeals the judges held that though none of the raiders were identified, the fingerprint evidence against the six was sufficient for the trial jury to infer they were plotters who also took part in the raid. In judgement it was said:

> Last year's £2,500,000 raid was warfare against society and an act of organized banditry touching new depths of lawlessness. In our judgement severe deterrent sentences are necessary to protect the community against these men for a long time.

Leave was refused for appeal to the House of Lords.

The next appeal against conviction and sentence was that of Douglas Goody, sentenced to 30 years' imprisonment. The Court of Criminal Appeal criticized irrelevant questions that Goody had

been asked at the trial. The questions were about Goody's acquittal at the Old Bailey last year in a case following a £65,000 bullion robbery at London Airport.

One of the judges said: 'No questions should have been asked about this matter. Still less should questions have been asked which had the effects of suggesting, even unintentionally, that Goody had been lucky to be acquitted.' Even if the court was satisfied there was such gross impropriety as to be likely to interfere with the trial, the conviction would not have been set aside.

Both the appeals were dismissed. Leave was refused for appeal to the House of Lords. Then followed the appeals of:

(a) Brian Arthur Field, sentenced to 25 years' imprisonment and 5 years' imprisonment concurrent for conspiracy to rob and conspiracy to obstruct justice.
(b) Leonard Denis Field, sentenced to 25 years' and 5 years' imprisonment concurrent for conspiracy to rob and conspiracy to obstruct justice.

The convictions and sentences in relation to the conspiracy to rob in both cases were quashed.

In judgement it was said that the trial jury at Aylesbury had acquitted Brian Arthur Field of receiving stolen money, even though two bags belonging to him were found full of banknotes at Dorking. Once dissociated from possession of any stolen money, the remaining facts against Brian Arthur Field were insufficient to enable the jury to infer he was guilty of conspiring to rob the mail train.

The judge said that Leonard Field, whom he described as 'a ready liar at the trial', was said to have investigated the purchase of Leatherslade Farm, the hideout of the robbers. No facts had been established that he knew of the intention to stop and rob the train.

information room should be properly recorded and adequate staff should always be available for this purpose.

(10) A sufficient staff was not readily available to carry out the necessary scenes of crime and fingerprint searches and to take photographs.

Recommendation. That the establishment of scenes of crime, fingerprint and photographic officers be reviewed.

(11) Within a few hours of the discovery of this crime a meeting was held in London of senior officials of all interested parties. This necessitated the chief constable and the detective superintendent, the two persons most vitally concerned with the police investigation, being absent from their force for a material time.

Recommendation. When it is necessary to have a conference of all interested parties during the early stages of the investigation of a serious crime, the conference should be held within the force area.

(12) At the meeting which was held in London on the afternoon of the 8th August, when important matters were discussed and decisions taken, no written record was made of these decisions.

Recommendation. That when any high-level conference is held with representatives of different organizations, minutes should be made and circulated to all who were present.

(13) Through lack of circulation of information through normal police channels, officers in the Buckinghamshire Constabulary and in surrounding forces were dependent on press reports for information about the crime.

Recommendation. When a serious crime is being investigated it should be the responsibility of a nominated officer to ensure that there is no delay in the circulation of necessary police messages.

(14) In an endeavour to 'flush' the thieves from their hideout the press were informed that the investigating officers had reason to believe that the thieves and loot were concealed within 30 miles of the scene of the crime. Nevertheless no action was taken to set up roadblocks and checkpoints so that the thieves might be intercepted if they did endeavour to move.

Recommendation. Before publicity is given to a particular aspect of a criminal investigation the officer in charge of the investigation should ensure that he has made adequate arrangements to deal with any possible results from the release of such information.

(15) When information was being sought about a likely hideout for the thieves no enquiries were made of local postmasters and sub-postmasters.

Recommendation. That investigating officers should realize the valuable information about the movement of persons which is in the possession of postmasters and sub-postmasters and that the assistance of these people should be sought if needs be through the Post Office Investigation Branch.

(16) At the commencement of the enquiry statements and reports were typed in quintuplicate by the use of carbons. When it was realized that more copies were required these statements and reports were re-typed on low-yield reproduction material. Eventually when it was realized that a large number of copies of each document would be required they were typed a third time on high-yield reproduction material.

Recommendation. When an enquiry of any magnitude is being commenced, all statements, reports, etc. should be typed on high-yield reproduction material.

(17) The safeguarding of prisoners during their appearance at court and during conveyance to and from prisons was extremely well carried out. Subsequent events, namely the

escape of Wilson from Winson Green Prison, Birmingham, now clearly indicates the care which is necessary to prevent this type of criminal from making an attempt to escape.
Recommendation. That an immediate review should be carried out respecting the facilities available for safeguarding prisoners appearing at courts.

(18) The same premises were used for the trial as were used for the committals and the same procedure was adopted in getting prisoners to court. Because of the temporary court arrangements, members of the jury and witnesses were able to see the arrival and departure of the prisoners. The precautions which had to be taken must obviously have indicated that the majority of the prisoners were known to be violent and experienced criminals. It is obviously undesirable that members of the jury should be prejudiced in this way.
Recommendation. The arrival of persons in custody at court should always be out of the view of the jury and witnesses.

(19) Senior Prosecuting Counsel made the opening speech, which commenced on 20th January and terminated on 22nd January. He found some difficulty in collating all the facts and stressed afterwards that in cases of this magnitude there was the need for an overall coordinator who had the complete picture of all that went on during the investigation. He found so often at briefings that it was necessary to go to a number of sources to discover points.
Recommendation. In the investigation of all serious crime there should be a police coordinator.

(20) It does not seem to have been appreciated by some of the officers engaged on this investigation that the judiciary have a right to exercise their discretion to admit evidence which appears to have been in breach of the Judges' Rules.

Recommendation. The existence of this discretion be brought to the notice of all police officers.

(21) The trials commenced on the 20th January 1964 and concluded on the 17th April 1964. This necessitated the use of police officers for guarding the prisoners, the judge and finally the jurymen and their homes. In addition a number of traffic points were manned several times a day. The public were thus deprived over a long period of many officers from normal duty. This placed an intolerable burden on the Buckinghamshire Constabulary. Aid should have been obtained from surrounding forces.

Recommendation. If duties are called for which are clearly beyond the resources of one force, mutual aid should be sought from surrounding forces.

(22) The resources of the Buckinghamshire Constabulary were taxed to the full. There were insufficient officers of real experience available from the outset to undertake the many enquiries. The availability of a district crime squad would have gone some way to overcome this difficulty.

Recommendation. A chief constable should not hesitate to ask for assistance from surrounding forces.

(23) Excellent work was done by the printing department at the Buckinghamshire Constabulary headquarters, which was equipped with up-to-date machines.

Recommendation. Proper facilities for printing should be available at all force headquarters.

(24) The increase of Flying Squad activities is realized when for the period from 9th August 1963 to 30th September 1963 they carried out 419 searches of premises as against 188 for the same period in 1962. This led to a number of arrests of persons not connected with the train robbery. This intensive action revealed itself as it gathered momentum, as serious

crime in London virtually stood still.

Recommendation. That CID establishment be increased so that this intensity of action be permanently maintained.

(25) Fingerprints were found at the scene of the crime and on articles which were subsequently recovered. Although some contained insufficient detail to establish the identity of any particular person they proved of great value to the finger-print experts when they were under cross-examination.

Recommendation. That photographs of all fingerprints or parts of fingerprints found at the scene of a crime, unless clearly identified as those of persons having legitimate access, should be made available to any fingerprint officer who is to give evidence in the case.

(26) Telephone calls from the press, coming into Buckingham-shire Constabulary headquarters during the early stages of the enquiry, continually blocked the lines. In the absence of a press liaison officer, pressmen developed the habit of wandering about the headquarters at Aylesbury. At times they were found in offices where confidential matters relating to the train robbery were being dealt with.

Recommendation. Headquarters of all police forces should have available ex-directory lines for use in emergency. When a serious crime or incident occurs a senior officer should be appointed immediately as the press liaison officer. This would leave investigators free from the concern of constant press pressure.

(27) The detective superintendent in charge of this enquiry indicated on the 16th March 1964 that he wished to retire on the 11th April 1964. On the 8th April he was interviewed by one of Her Majesty's Inspectors of Constabulary in the presence of his own chief constable. In reply to a question he admitted that he had already written an article of between 50

and 60,000 words touching on the investigation of this serious crime and that he had already handed this article to the press. An edited version of this article was published in two instalments in a Sunday newspaper on the 19th and 26th April 1964. It will be remembered that when the detective superintendent retired on the 11th April this enquiry was not complete. Much of the stolen money had not been recovered and three notorious criminals were still being sought. *Recommendation.* That a police officer be prohibited from publishing articles relating to cases which he has handled or of which he has obtained knowledge by virtue of his service in the police, without the consent of the chief officer of police under whom he was serving at the time of his retirement.

●●●

The following are some of the more interesting features:

(1) The successful handling of such a large number of exhibits resulted from the wisdom of making one officer responsible for collecting, recording and labelling them from the very outset.

(2) It was fortunate that there was a comparatively new police headquarters at Aylesbury and that without unduly prejudicing ordinary routine police work accommodation could be made available for the setting up of an incident room, exhibits room, documents room and an office for the officer in charge of the investigation. The availability of sleeping and catering facilities also proved invaluable.

(3) The 'intelligence' produced by the Criminal Intelligence Bureau COC11 at New Scotland Yard proved to be

remarkably accurate. This comparatively new department fully justified its existence so far as this investigation was concerned.

(4) A practice was adopted when premises were to be searched of having a member of the Metropolitan Police Forensic Science Laboratory present. This proved vital on one occasion when certain inferences were made at the trial and dispelled in connection with the prisoner Goody and the paint found on his shoes.

(5) Appeals were made through the press, radio and television respecting persons wanted by the police in connection with the train robbery. Accurate records were kept as to the extent the news relating to wanted persons was circulated, with a list of names of persons who could if necessary give evidence of particulars appearing in various publications. In cross-examination, much use was made of the knowledge that this evidence was readily available.

(6) Use of *Police Five* was wisely made respecting the three vehicles seen on the Cublington–Aston Abbotts road.

(7) It was as a result of a conference in Hertfordshire that a message was circulated at 10.30 a.m. 12th August 1963, asking for enquiries of estate agents relating to transactions in connection with farms within a 30-mile radius of Cheddington. The value of the suggestion relating to the enquiries at estate agents was realized, particularly when it was known that Leatherslade Farm had been up for sale since February or March 1963. This clearly indicated the value of conferring with the senior officers of a surrounding force.

(8) Despite lack of information but realizing the magnitude of the offence, the surrounding counties of Hertfordshire, Bedfordshire and Oxfordshire all took positive action, mostly of their own initiative. Oxfordshire offered the loan of

uniformed and Criminal Investigation Department officers but the offer was not taken up. Bedfordshire if approached would also have been willing to loan men. It is suggested that when any major crime occurs, consideration should be given to asking for mutual aid from surrounding forces and in addition to hold conferences with those forces to pool ideas.

(9) Police public address equipment was used to make announcements in 17 villages in the locality of Leatherslade Farm. The information which resulted from this action was of value.

(10) The first two arrests were made by Bournemouth Police. The prisoners were searched there and their property logged. It was alleged at the trial that the property found on the prisoners Boal and Cordrey had been mixed when they were searched and there was some question as to which prisoner was in possession of certain keys when arrested. The system adopted by Bournemouth when prisoners are searched was examined, which showed that the prisoners were searched individually and their property kept separate. It is most important that when two or more prisoners are arrested together their property is kept separate.

(11) Due to the large amount of monies recovered and knowing that some of it may well be identified bank officials were given the task of counting and examining it.

(12) A man, subsequently identified as James Edward White, CRO 26113/35, and still wanted in connection with the train robbery, was checked but not detained by two police constables at Reigate, Surrey, on the 13th August 1963, as a result of a complaint from a shopkeeper. White had not been circulated as wanted at this time. The number of his car was noted and it was as a result of this that further enquiries were made by the Surrey Constabulary, the caravan at Boxhill was

located and other evidence collected which helped to connect White with the robbery. Little blame can be attached to the officers who saw White in allowing him to go as they had virtually nothing at that time to connect him with the robbery.

(13) Nothing can be overlooked when premises are searched. A hotel bill found at the house of one prisoner was examined for fingerprints. On it was found the fingerprint of another prisoner which proved a definite connection.

(14) A number of the prisoners when seen denied all knowledge of Leatherslade Farm or Cheddington. These denials were noted and proved useful later in cross-examination, particularly as evidence had been given that their fingerprints had been found at the farm.

(15) A fingerprint found on a bank authority definitely established the identity of the prospective purchaser of Leatherslade Farm as Leonard Denis Field.

(16) Fingerprints on a briefcase containing stolen money found with other cases in a Surrey wood, together with a hotel bill found in the lining of one of the cases, when properly checked definitely established the ownership of these cases and connected them with one of the prisoners. This again illustrates the value of examining thoroughly property coming into the possession of the police in connection with crime.

(17) The complicated enquiry into the prospective purchase of Leatherslade Farm was undertaken by the Metropolitan and City Police Company Fraud Squad, whose expert knowledge proved the undoing of Wheater, a fact well worth bearing in mind when enquiries of a similar nature have to be made.

(18) The 'Pipkin' can on which Welch's palmprint was found had the number '723' stamped on top. The fact this was taken

special extension was installed at the Criminal Record Office for 'urgent name' searches to be made during the course of the trial. A room was set aside at the court in which two telephones had been installed. This enabled liaison to be maintained between the London end and Aylesbury. An officer was also available to act as a 'runner' between the court and the incident room.

(24) The problem of finding a court large enough to accommodate the prisoners' Counsel, other officers of the court, and the public and how this was overcome at Aylesbury was described.

(25) A press reporter was subpoenaed to give evidence for one of the prisoners. This illustrates the danger of some pressmen and the value of appointing an authorized police/press liaison officer in all cases of serious crime to prevent leakages of information to the press.

(26) The day before the termination of the trial a juror was approached by a man and asked to sway the jury, for a consideration, as some of his friends were on trial. This was brought to the notice of the judge.

(27) The accommodation of the jury after retirement and the method of communication between the jury room and Buckinghamshire Constabulary headquarters, was considered. 'Walkie-talkie' apparatus was used.

(28) The Flying Squad at New Scotland Yard was active from the start. An incident room was set up there to deal exclusively with the collating and logging of information received in connection with the train robbery.

(29) The adequate guarding of Leatherslade Farm proved invaluable when fingerprint evidence was being given at the trial.

(30) The fingerprint experts were necessary to examine the fingerprints *in situ* and to develop them.

(31) When a crime is committed which involves GPO property, as in this case, it is advisable to liaise with them to the full. The GPO were in a position to loan 30 men to assist on various aspects of the investigation. They also set up an incident room at GPO Headquarters, London, to channel information.

(32) Close liaison with the GPO on this enquiry resulted in additional telephones being installed when required immediately.

(33) Consultation with the GPO when charges were being framed in connection with theft of their property proved invaluable.

(34) The GPO Investigation Branch were asked for full details of ticketed telephone calls from the homes of the accused; these were to be used to help prove the conspiracy. After reporting that no calls had been made from Brian Field's house, the GPO were asked to check again and this produced a list of calls whilst the trial was in progress. This was probably a small administrative failure but further points to the need for an overall coordinator in major enquiries to see that the investigation programme is pushed along.

(35) As a result of the close liaison between the interested parties, British Transport Police supplied 21 detective officers. This greatly assisted as they made all enquiries relating to railway personnel at stations at which the train stopped before reaching the scene of the attack. In addition they made enquiries respecting the use of the reserve HVP coach and the fact that three HVP coaches were out of action. Their expert knowledge of the internal working of British Railways was invaluable.

(36) The British Transport Police set up an incident room at their headquarters at Park Royal, London NW10, through which all railway enquiries were channelled either to Aylesbury or

New Scotland Yard. This was another valuable lesson.

(37) Despite suggestions made that a number of HVP coaches were out of action and that there was a possibility of sabotage, nothing was found to support this.

(38) Close liaison with the assessors is worth bearing in mind. When large rewards are offered they often come into possession of information invaluable to the enquiry.

HMI

6th October 1964

POSTSCRIPT

The three robbers who were being sought when the foregoing report was submitted to the Home Office in 1964 were eventually brought to justice: James White and Bruce Reynolds were arrested in England and 'Buster' Edwards returned voluntarily from Mexico. Charles Wilson and Ronald Biggs, who escaped from prison in, respectively, 1964 and 1965, were re-arrested – the first in 1968, the second in 2001.

James White was arrested at his home in Kent – where he and his wife had been living quietly under assumed names – in April 1966 and was tried two months later at Leicester Assizes. He handed over the £2,000 found in his possession and told the police about £6,000 hidden in a house trailer. White pleaded guilty to robbery, and the Prosecution accepted his plea of not guilty to conspiracy. Sentenced to 18 years' imprisonment, he was released after nine years and went into the building business.

After spending some time in Germany, **Ronald ('Buster') Edwards** fled to Mexico with his wife and daughter in March 1965. Largely in view of White's more lenient sentence, he gave himself up in September 1966.

Tried at Nottinghamshire Assizes the following December, Edwards was sentenced to 12 years' imprisonment for conspiracy to rob and a concurrent term of 15 years for robbery. The judge said:

> You have been convicted on overwhelming evidence of a crime which shocked every person in this country. You played for high stakes and punishment must, in the public interest, be severe. I deal with you on the footing that you were in on this at a very early stage indeed, but nevertheless that you were not one of the leading planners, or a dealer in the matter at all. I deal with it on

The scene outside Wandsworth prison the day after Ronald Biggs escaped in July 1965. He jumped through a hole in the roof of the furniture van and went out of the back of the van into a waiting car.

the footing that you were, in the hierarchy – if that is the proper word to use – somewhere below White.

Released in 1975, Edwards became a flower seller outside Waterloo station. He hanged himself in 1994.

Bruce Reynolds went to France in August 1964, to Mexico in November 1964 with his wife and son, to Canada in 1966, back to the south of France and returned to London in 1968. He was arrested in Torquay in November 1968 and tried at the old Assize Court in Aylesbury in January 1969. He pleaded guilty and expressed contrition. His defence counsel reminded the judge that Bruce had enabled the police to recover £5,500 of the stolen money. Sentencing Bruce, the judge said:

> It would be wrong for me to give any encouragement to the idea that successful avoidance of arrest for a period entitles a criminal to a reduction in sentence. ... I shall make the same kind of reduction in sentence as I believe would, in like circumstances, have been made by the judge at the main trial. I sentence you to 25 years' imprisonment.

Reynolds was released after 10 years.

Charles Wilson was abducted from prison on August 1964 and in March of the following year went to the south of France. In November 1965 he was in Mexico City and shortly afterwards went to Canada, where he was joined by his wife and daughters. He was arrested there in January 1968 and served a further 10 years in the high-security wing at Parkhurst on the Isle of Wight. On his release he went to Marbella in Spain. He was shot dead by a hitman on bicycle in 1990.

Wilson photographed by Montreal police in January 1968, shortly before his deportation to England

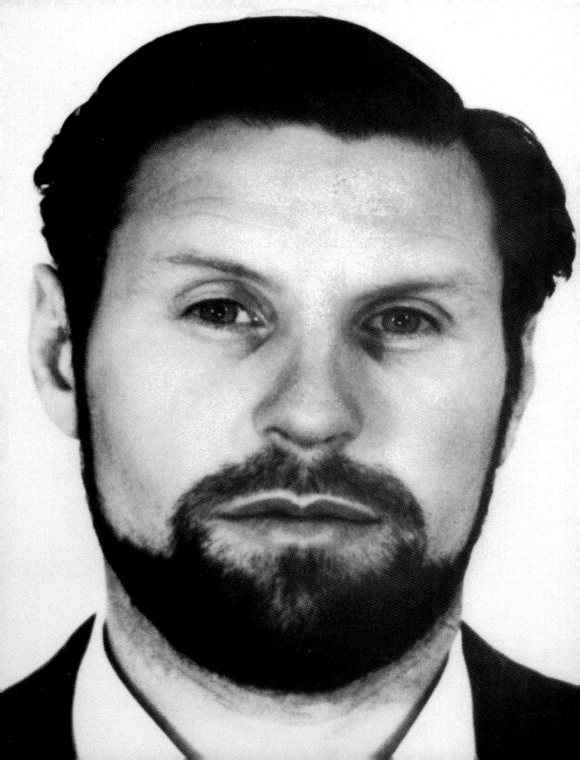

Ronald Biggs escaped from Wandsworth in July 1965. In October 1965 he was in France (where he had plastic surgery in Paris) and in December 1965 in Australia. In January 1970 he decided to move to Brazil. Almost 36 years after his escape, aged 71, he returned voluntarily to the UK. Three hours after his arrival he was back in the dock and returned to jail to complete his 30-year sentence.

In all, members of the gang were sentenced to a total of 300 years. £2,295,150 of the amount stolen was never recovered by the insurance adjusters. Much of it was spent on the robbers' legal expenses; a sizeable amount was spent 'on the run'; some was left with 'minders'. Whether there is any hidden hoard remains a matter for speculation.

May 6, 2001: Ronald Biggs at Rio de Janeiro Airport, on his way back to England after an exile of 31 years in Brazil

Moments of History

2002

The Irish Book of Death and Flying Ships
Marilyn Monroe: the FBI files

2003

The British War in Afghanistan
Escaping from Germany: the British Government files
The Great British Train Robbery, 1963
The Highland Division by Eric Linklater
John Lennon: the FBI files
The Mediterranean Fleet: Greece to Tripoli
The Scandal of Christine Keeler and John Profumo: Lord Denning's Report, 1963
The Shooting of John F. Kennedy, 1963: The Warren Commission

2004

Florence Nightingale
Nixon and Watergate
Peace in Tibet: the Younghusband expedition, 1904
Sacco and Vanzetti: the FBI files
The Theft of the Irish Crown Jewels, 1907
Victory in Europe, 1945: General Eisenhower's Report
War in Italy, 1944: the battles for Monte Cassino
Worldwide Battles of the Great War, 1915–1918

Uncovered Editions

Crime

Rillington Place, 1949
The Strange Story of Adolf Beck
The Trials of Oscar Wilde, 1895

Also in the news in 1963 (clockwise from top right): Christine Keeler, The Beatles, *The Great Escape* with Steve McQueen, John F. Kennedy and family. Related *Moments of History* titles are *The Scandal of Christine Keeler and John Profumo, John Lennon: the FBI files, Escaping from Germany, The Shooting of John F. Kennedy*

The War Facsimiles

(Illustrated books published by the British government during the war years)
The Battle of Britain, August–October 1940
The Battle of Egypt, 1942
Bomber Command, September 1939–July 1941
East of Malta, West of Suez, September 1939 to March 1941
Fleet Air Arm, 1943
Land at War, 1939–1944
Ocean Front: the story of the war in the Pacific, 1941–1944
Roof over Britain, 1939–1942

World War I

British Battles of World War I, 1914–15
Defeat at Gallipoli: the Dardanelles Commission Part II, 1915–16
Lord Kitchener and Winston Churchill: the Dardanelles Commission Part I,
    1914–15
The Russian Revolution, 1917
War 1914: Punishing the Serbs
The World War I Collection (Dardanelles Commission, British Battles of World
    War I)

World War II

Attack on Pearl Harbor, 1941
D Day to VE Day: General Eisenhower's Report, 1944–45
Escape from Germany, 1939–45
The Judgment of Nuremberg, 1946
Tragedy at Bethnal Green
War 1939: Dealing with Adolf Hitler
The World War II Collection (War 1939, D Day to VE Day, Judgment of
    Nuremberg)
(see also *The War Facsimiles*)

UK Distribution and Orders

Littlehampton Book Services, Faraday Close, Durrington, West Sussex BN13 3RB
Telephone: 01903 828800 Fax: 01903 828801
E-mail: orders@lbsltd.co.uk

Sales Representation

Compass Independent Book Sales, Barley Mow Centre, 10 Barley Mow Passage,
Chiswick, London W4 4PH
Telephone: 0208 994 6477 Fax: 0208 400 6132

US Sales and Distribution

Midpoint Trade Books, 27 West 20th Street, Suite 1102, New York, NY 10011
Telephone: (1) 212 727 0190 Fax: (1) 212 727 0195

Midpoint Trade Books, 1263 Southwest Blvd, Kansas City, KS 66103
Telephone: (1) 913 831 2233 Fax: (1) 913 362 7401

Other Representation
Australia

Nick Walker, Australian Book Marketing/Australian Scholarly Publishing Pty Ltd
PO Box 299, Kew, Victoria 3101; Suite 102, 282 Collins Street, Melbourne 3000
Telephone: 03 9654 0250 Fax: 03 9663 0161
E-mail: aspec@ozemail.com.au

Scandinavia

Hanne Rotovnik, Publishers' Representative, Taarbaek PO Box 5, Strandvej 59 0,
DK-2930 Klampenborg
E-mail: Hanne@rotovnik.dk

South Africa

Colin McGee, Stephan Phillips (Pty) Ltd. PO Box 434, Umdloti Beach 4350
Telephone: +27 (0) 31 568 2902 Fax: +27 (0) 31 568 2922
E-mail: colinmcgee@mweb.co.za

Titles can also be ordered from www.timcoatesbooks.com